Psychotherapy and the
Behavioral Sciences

Psychotherapy and the Behavioral Sciences

CONTRIBUTIONS OF THE BIOLOGICAL, PSYCHOLOGICAL, SOCIAL AND PHILOSOPHIC FIELDS TO PSYCHOTHERAPEUTIC THEORY AND PROCESS

LEWIS R. WOLBERG, M.D.

Dean and Medical Director, Postgraduate Center for Mental Health, and Clinical Professor of Psychiatry, New York Medical College, New York, N.Y.

GRUNE & STRATTON, *New York and London*

Contents

Preface

DURING THE PAST TWO DECADES AN INFORMATION EXPLOSION HAS rocked the foundations of every science dealing with man. It has added vital data to our stores of knowledge, stimulating exciting protocols and posing new hypotheses. In the cauldron of this pansophical ferment, the field of psychotherapy has found sustenance. Observations from the growing specialties of neurophysiology, biochemistry, genetics, ethology, conditioning theory, developmental theory, personality theory, learning theory, psychoanalysis, social theory, role theory, group dynamics, cultural anthropology, information theory, communications theory, cybernetics, philosophy and field theory have slowly filtered into the provinces of the helping professions. Since psychotherapists are increasingly borrowing precepts and suppositions, as well as methods from disciplines related to the biological and social sciences, it is only proper that they possess an understanding of how material from these sciences may best be amalgamated with their own theories, as well as the effect and validity of such cross fertilization. Lines along which psychotherapy may be enriched will then more clearly come to light. It is the purpose of this volume to outline some of the contributions from, and new developments in, the various fields with which psychotherapy is affiliated, and to indicate their influence on certain contemporary trends in psychotherapeutic theory and process.

LEWIS R. WOLBERG
1966

I

Neurophysiological Approaches

THE MIND, SAID STANLEY COBB (1958), IS A FUNCTION OF THE brain in action. Although physiologists have always known that the essence of mental function is embedded in brain structure, it is only recently, with the refinement of our investigative tools, that a demonstration of the relationship has been possible, thus bringing the physiology and chemistry of the brain within the bounds of interest of the psychotherapist. The importance of this knowledge for the therapist lies in the understanding he can gain regarding the physiological manifestations of emotion and the rationale of, and indications for, the adjunctive uses of the somatic therapies. It enables him to comprehend some of the workings of the nervous system, and perhaps to coordinate this knowledge with psychotherapeutic theory and practice.

The work of Sherrington (1936) on levels of nervous integration, of Bianchi (1920) on neural mechanisms and functions of the frontal lobes in experimental animals, of Pavlov (1928) on conditioning, of Magoun (1954) on the reticular activating system, of Papez (1937) on the limbic system, of Penfield (1951) on electrical brain stimulation, and of the Vogts (1951) on physiological mapping of the cerebral cortex have been particularly important in providing a foundation for our present-day efforts in correlating mind with brain.

Advances in histochemistry, biophysics, electrophysiology, electroencephalography, histometabolism, electron microscopy, X-ray diffraction, historadioautography, and microabsorption spectrophotometry enable us to study the physiological processes within nerve cells, the integrated activities of neurones, the mapping of cerebral areas, and the organization of the myelo-, cyto-, and angioarchitecture of the brain. These investigations have opened new vistas in harmonizing physiological and psychological relation-

1

ships. Out of such observations has emerged an understanding that "mind" is "not a single, total, indivisible function of the entire brain but a composite of numerous partial functions, most of which were related to distinct areas of the cerebral cortex and subcortical regions as well as being variously interconnected among themselves" (Roizin, 1959). The old conception of localized function in brain centers has been replaced by an understanding of the dynamic localization of functions. It has been possible not only to establish the consociation between disturbances in function and structure in conditions in which neuropathology is demonstrably obvious, such as circulatory disorders, focal infections, degenerative conditions, toxic states, and neoplastic diseases, but also to elaborate related hypotheses regarding pathological sites and modes of operation of psychoneurotic and psychotic afflictions in which no physical alterations are discernible with our present-day instruments. Freud's early prediction that "all our provisional ideas on psychology will some day be based on organic structure" may through these studies some day come to realization.

A number of contemporary problems hamper this objective. First, physiological doctrines are as ill-defined and debatable as the psychological structures which they presume to explain. Second, a reduction of behavioral data into smaller observable units which may be measured; the reasoning applicable to such units then being applied to larger structures, such as behavior as a whole, results in inferences that do not always hold up under close scrutiny. Nevertheless, employment of the experimental methods of the physical sciences to the problems of human behavior has yielded some interesting leads. We are now more capable than ever before of developing empirical generalizations that structure the relationship between organic, behavioral and environmental variables. It is even predicted that our growing knowledge of brain physiology will enable us in the not too distant future to influence behavior change more effectively by applying electrochemical processes directly on specific tissue areas than by our present-day diffuse verbal and other external sensory conditioning stimuli (Franks, 1965). Considerable progress has been made toward this end with the introduction of psychoactive drugs, refinements in electroconvulsive therapy, and experiments involving selected brain surgery. Such developments, still in a pioneer stage, offer promise of revolutionary changes in our approach to emotional illness. At the present time they contribute important adjunctive help toward the management of severe mental ailments.

The neuronal building blocks. It is impossible to understand the operations of the nervous system without considering the functions of the individual building blocks, the neurons. These, numbering a million billion, are organized in complex and highly integrated assemblies for the passage of information from the world surrounding the individual to the innermost parts of his body, and, conversely, from the remotest regions within to the external limits of the environment. Modern neurological research has opened the door to many of the ongoing processes of this stupendous army of neurons. But the mysteries still to be solved vastly outnumber the facts about which we are certain.

Essentially the neuron is a complex, highly organized structure capable of intricate metabolic, biophysical and bioelectric activities which sponsor the assimilation, storage, utilization and, upon stimulation, discharge of energy to the synaptic field with which its axon is affiliated. These reception, conduction and discharge functions are vitally influenced by the specific molecular organization, and the biochemical and enzymic requirements of a particular neuron. The consequences of neuronal activity depend on the kinds of anatomical connections and synaptic relationships of the networks of which a neuron is a part. A good deal of the neuronal activity is accounted for in the reactions of the synapses. While the architecture of the synapse is still unclear, as are its exact physical, chemical and electrical constituents, there is little question that it significantly alters the input and the distribution of impulses. There is evidence that the synapse is conditioned by previous messages so that it responds more readily to those to which it has already been subjected.

Neuronal nuclei generate electrical energy which traverse their axons and synaptic terminals across which they discharge themselves to adjoining nerve or muscle cells. Studies indicate that the transmission of impulses across the nerve endings, and probably through the entire nerve fiber, is related to actions of the chemical acetylcholine, manufactured and split up within the body by special enzymes. Acetylcholine is presumably combined with the receptor protein to alter its permeability to the passage of positive sodium ions, temporarily changing the electrical potential of the neuron and inducing an electrical impulse. Within thirty- or forty-millionths of a second after acetylcholine acts, it is destroyed by the enzyme cholinesterase. There are some authorities who believe that inhibited synaptic function in the neurons of the brain is a principal factor in mental disease. Adrenergic substances, like epinephrine (adrenalin), LSD-25, serotonin and mescaline, by exercising an inhibiting effect on the synapse, have been implicated as factors in mental disease. On the other hand, acetylcholine (stimulated by certain psychotropic drugs which have an adrenergic blocking effect) stimulates synaptic transmission and is said to be associated with the relief of mental symptoms.

The threshold of a neuron which determines whether or not it will fire depends upon the intensity of incoming nerve messages, the metabolic state of the soma, and the chemical and electrical field in which the neuron is operating. The soma may be excited or inhibited by stimuli which change the threshold to excitation, perhaps by increasing or decreasing the membrane and somatic potentials. Neurohumoral transmitter substances (acetylcholine and histamine) and electrical currents play a role in this process. When excitatory influences exceed the excitatory threshold, the neuron will fire. Inhibitory impulses raise the threshold to a point where the cell will resist stimulation. This may be an important factor in neuroses and psychoses.

Conduction of impulses in the neuron is dependent on the macromolecule miscelles in the axon surface which chemically arrange themselves as a result of stimulation during the development and life of the cell. Experience imprints itself on the neuron in the form of a subcellular change, which influences the generation and flow of nerve impulses. Functional rearrangements within a cell can result in structural molecular alterations leading to a changed system of interconnective assemblies, chains and loops. Intricate behavior patterns are the product of these complex circuits which become responsible for a rich repertoire of behavioral responses.

Pathological functioning of the neurons may occur as a result of varied conditions within the brain including those that accompany prolonged stress. Reactions to strong stimuli become weaker, and to weak stimuli paradoxically stronger. A diffuse, generalized irradiation of excitement may eventuate. Extraneous stimuli readily disrupt the established system of connections. The equilibrium between excitation and inhibition in the higher cortical centers become disorganized with a consequent overexaggeration of responses or with abnormal reactions of sluggishness or torpor. Mobility of reaction, which enables a person rapidly to inhibit certain systems of connections and to pass to others, is lost.

The memory trace. The brain is a bundle of neuronal structures that mediates consciousness, thinking, emotional reactions, and motor behavior. It is the reservoir for the storage of vast amounts of information, and for the coordination of this information in pursuit of problem solving. A massive recording system, it retains a permanent record of what has passed through its constituent neurons.

Storage elements in the brain are extensively dispersed so that auditory, visual, tactile, olfactory, gustatory, and other experiences occurring outside and within the body are fixated over widespread areas, but are associatively tied together by neuronal interconnections. The loss of one area by brain damage does not necessarily effect the associations in other areas. It is quite likely that there is some reduplication of stored memory traces, and that the bilateral lobes of the brain operate in tandem.

It has been estimated that in a single lifetime fifteen trillion bits of information pour into the brain to be received, processed and stored by its ten billion cells. The memory trace is probably registered in the complex protein molecules (ribonucleic acid— RNA) of the nerve cell, which encodes the information and transmits it through the cell body, axon, and across the synapse to other neurons. The exact place where the trace is recorded is not known. Some consider its location the soma; others the interface between the neuronal and glial tissues. At any rate neurons and glia operate as a functional unit, the glia apparently supplying the substrate for the neuron during enhanced nerve activity which is used to increase the output of RNA and proteins. Every particle of protein contains an enormous amount of stored information, estimated at 8×10^8 *in each molecule* (Bell, 1962). When we consider that the storage capacity of the largest computer is only 5×10^6, the depository resources of the brain appear staggering.

The degree and permanence of molecular reorganization in the neurons are dependent to a large extent on the intensity of the original stimulation. The cerebral cortex exercises highly selected screening toward incoming stimuli. The cerebral cortex also particularizes which memories will be released. Obviously only a tiny fraction of the total mnemonic pool can be allowed entry into awareness. Under ordinary circumstances, where healthy conditions prevail, the neuronal circuits utilized, which contain the etchings of experience, are goal directed, serving the purpose of adaptation. In pathological states certain memory releases become chaotic, and, while they may fulfill some subversive function, they detract from, rather than add to, the adjustment potential.

There is evidence that important memories, once stored, and their associated emotions and action tendencies, are not extinguished easily, even though they lay dormant in the psyche. Hypothetically the reason may be that such memories are being reinforced daily, satisfying random inner needs not apparent on the surface. Whether this be true or not, residues of the entire past life are latently available to the individual in their pristine form. Penfield (1952), applying electrical charges to the temporal cortex exposed during a brain operation, was able to elicit in his patients not only vivid memories of past experiences, but the emotions originally associated with the experiences, and the same interpretations, true or false, that had previously been given to the experiences. The memory when it was evoked was "as clear as it would have been thirty seconds after the original experience." For example, one patient, upon stimulation of the same area twenty times, heard a popular song each time which began with the verse and went on to the chorus, and was so vivid that she imagined it came from a record player in the adjoining room. Employing hypnosis and the psychotomimetic drugs, clinicians often demonstrate that remote memories of past activities and their associations are vividly reactivated.

The executive neocortex. Thinking may be conceived of neurophysiologically as the product of electrical impulses coursing through the multiple synaptic connections of cortical neurons with their ramified dendritic networks, circumscribed by the selective discrimination of multiform subcortical influences, as well as of intracortical associative excitations.

The function of the cerebral cortex (neocortex) with its capacities for reasoning and judgement is essentially a supervisory one; monitoring the relationship of the individual with the environment, selecting stimuli for storage, coordinating stored information with present reality, organizing action tendencies to supply inner needs, and satisfying contingencies essential for bodily homeostasis—in short, providing the ways and means for the survival of the individual and the species. Directing stimuli over various pathways of the neuronal network, abstracting, integrating and fusing past and present experiences, and sending excitatory and inhibitory impulses through nerve fibers and synapses at a rate estimated at 500 per second at the height of a response, the cortex is capable of focusing attention on aspects of inner and outer experience. While conscious cortical operations are not always essential to establish enduring memory patterns, they do facilitate the recording and arrangement of memories in proper perspective. Volitional remembering is a product of cortical awareness. Finally, the cortex is capable of effectuating generalizations, facilitating prehension, apperception, learning, and inferential reasoning. How these miracles of mentation are accomplished, what constitutes "willing," cogitation, insight and other sophisticated pursuits of the mind, are still beyond our present capacities for understanding and must await the discoveries of neurophysiologists of the future.

Much of human superability is fostered by man's orientation to reality through language. Words, through conditioning, systematize impressions, and embody and express social experience. The organization of words into language constitutes the foundation of thinking, and adds to the mobility of nervous processes and the regulation of motor reactions. Behavior is then subordinated to verbally formulated intentions. Words may influence, direct and alter various kinds of lower level functions (Luria, 1959 a, b).

Some attempts have been made to study the mechanisms of the cortex by surgical operations, removing different lobes or severing the connections of lobes from the rest of the brain. The consequence of these experiments has been an accumulation of evidence of the vertical organization of the central nervous system, extensive connections existing between higher and lower centers. Apparent also is the finding that brain functions are controlled by numerous interlocking circuits tying together different brain levels. Pathological phenomena resulting from ablation experiments have opened the door to an understanding of the operations of various cortical zones. Thus removal of the frontal lobe (lobectomy) releases inhibitions, alters time associations, and promotes a change in personality characterized by poor judgement, irritability, relaxation, euphoria and some intellectual defect. Removal of both temporal lobes leads to indifference, facetiousness and difficulties in apperception, memory and orientation. Ablation of the parietal cortex produces defects in intellectual comprehension and in the intrapsychic representation of the world and the self. The effects of frontal cortical ablation have led to the employment of surgical procedures to control certain mental and emotional disturbances. For example, sectioning of pathways to the frontal cortex from deeper areas, such as from the thalamus, or removal of selected areas (lobotomy, leucotomy) have been found helpful in some chronic and presumably incurable schizophrenic conditions and in unyielding anxiety states associated with chronic obsessive-compulsive neurosis.

Stimulation of the cut end of the vagus nerve has revealed increased electrical potentials in the inferior portion of the frontal lobe. This would seem to point to the orbital surface of the frontal lobe as the cortical projection terminus of afferent fibers of the vagus nerve, and perhaps account for the cortical influence on the viscera and for the conditioning of internal physiological functions to words and other symbols. Thus autonomic (sympathetic and parasympathetic) patterns may be mobilized by symbols of danger situations (perceptions, words, thoughts, memories, etc.) even though the original conditionings are outside of immediate awareness, having been forgotten or repressed. There is abundant evidence from animal and human brain experimentation, and from clinical studies, that trauma in the brain may induce visceral disease; for example, certain brain lesions may lead to peptic ulcer. Stimulation of the brain can result in major elevations in blood lipids with the development of aortic atheroma (Gunn, et al., 1960). These effects are evidence of the "basic importance of the brain in the body's myriad regulating processes" (S. Wolf, 1963).

Emotional activities, too, undoubtedly embrace the cortex, even though they may originate in subcortical areas. The thalamus and particularly its medial dorsal nucleus, which represents the primitive brain, makes extensive connections to the forebrain involving the cortex in coordinated high level functions related to the awareness of anxiety and pain, self-consciousness, creative imagination and language elaboration (Papez, 1959). The hippocampal gyrus attaches to the lingual gyrus and the gyrus back of the corpus callosum. Transcortical impressions from the upper brain are thus integrated in the hippocampal gyrus and modified to form emotional moods flavoring states of love, hate, sexual feeling, fight, flight, and various likes and dislikes. The outer layers of the cortex also are bound through the internal capsule to the reticular formation of the brain stem and nuclei of the thalamus, transmitting cortical impulses to, and receiving visceral-reticular stimuli from, the reticular activating system in a constant feedback, resulting in a unity of responses to complex messages.

The reticular integrator and brain energizer. A mass of cells in the brain stem and spinal column, inherited from our vertebrate ancestors, the *reticular formation* acts as an internuncial pathway, and, by influencing both sensory input and motor output the entire length of the neuraxis, it exercises control over autonomic and neuromuscular functions. Moreover the brain stem reticular formation (in the bulb, pons and mesencephalon) together with the subthalamus, hypothalamus and ventromedial part of the thalamus, acts as a kind of power plant, sending impulses to the cerebral cortex through diffuse projective fibers constituting the *reticular activating system*. The consequence of this stimulation is an alerting reaction believed to be responsible for the maintenance of consciousness. In turn the system is influenced by the cerebral cortex. Dulling the reticular activating system by shutting out stimuli reduces its effect on the cortex and results in relaxation and ultimately sleep. Drugging it with anesthetics produces anesthesia and stupor. Destroying it surgically leads to permanent coma. The system receives stimuli from all parts of the sensory apparatus, and responds by imparting to them an emotional cloak. Sending impulses down the spine, it influences visceral regulatory mechanisms, muscle tone and movement. In short, the reticular activating system is vitally important in stimulating the cerebral cortex (affecting awareness, attention, comprehension and probably the learning process itself), in innervating the limbic system (fermenting emotional expression) in exciting the hypothalamus (provoking the endocrine and autonomic systems) and, in concert with the cerebral cortex, controlling behavior in general. Being highly susceptible to drugs and neurohumors, the system may be studied to investigate some of the physiological roots of regressive behavior as well as to determine the effect on behavior of psychochemical agents which stimulate or depress it.

The emotional circuit of Papez (limbic system; rhinencephalon; hippocampal system). Derived from the embryonic olfactory structure, and often referred to as "man's visceral brain" because it dominates his emotional behavior and superintends the activity of the autonomic nervous system, the limbic system is closely related, functionally and anatomically, to the reticular activating system, influencing and in turn being influenced by the cerebral cortex and the hypothalamus. The system, in harmony with the cerebral cortex, administers the synergy of emotional reactions with behavioral responses, the mediation of bodily needs and visceral reactions (like sex and hunger) and the coordination of crude awareness with discriminating consciousness. The system is activated by stimuli reaching the hippocampus and the amygdala. Impulses are then passed through the fornix, the mammillary bodies of the hypothalamus, anterior thalamic nuclei, and finally reach the brain cortex in the cingulate gyrus. Fibers from the cingulate gyrus in turn connect with the hippocampus permitting a feedback of stimuli. The system regulates innate, automatized reactions associated with fight, flight, sex, feeding, searching and emotionally provoking situations. The hippocampus is believed to be crucially necessary for normal learning and memory.

Each of the constituent members of the limbic system contributes a distinctive component to the total reaction. Some attempt has been made to determine the specific role of different regions by local chemical and electrical stimulation and by ablation. Thus stimulating the septum, hippocampus and cingulate gyrus of monkeys and cats, produces grooming and sexual responses, while ablation may bring forth hypersexuality as well as bizarre sexual reactions. It is interesting that this part of the anatomy is affiliated with the sense of smell. We know clinically that a relationship exists between sex and odors. Stimulation of the amygdaloid nuclei in cats produces lesions in the gastric mucosa akin to peptic ulcer. Damage to the amygdala or cingulate gyrus will make a wild animal tame; while damage to the septum brings out rage in even well trained creatures. In humans destroying the amygdala can produce intense sexual feeling; resulting in satyriasis and nymphomania; while stimulation of the amygdala generates violent anger and occasionally terror and pain. Electrical stimuli applied to some areas of the limbic system will produce fear and anger, as well as fight and flight responses similar to those provoked by stimulating the posterior hypothalamus. On the other hand animals with implanted electrodes in other areas of the system will work at a self-stimulating machine to exhaustion, since the effects of stimulation are apparently pleasurable. The exact meaning of such varied phenomena is not entirely clear, but it is apparent that psychological and physiological reactions are closely intertwined, with a ceaseless feedback so that psychological processes (and words as conditioned stimuli) influence physiological reactions, and physiological reactions in turn promote psychological responses. Bound together in interacting circuits are the cerebral cortex (neocortex), reticular activating system, limbic system, and hypothalamus which participate together in the production and expression of emotion. The "feeling" part of emotion is believed to be located in the limbic system, while the "knowing" part is centered in the neocortex. Transcortical impressions from various brain areas—visual, auditory, olfactory, parietal, uncinate—and afferent impulses from the viscera are relayed to the hippocampal gyrus to the limbic system where they are integrated. Experimental observations implicate the limbic system in the excretion of ACTH and sex hormones.

The hypothalamic regulator of homeostasis. Closely affiliated with the emotional circuit is the hypothalamus, a key structure in regulating the internal environment, crucially influencing and in turn being influenced by higher level psychological activities. Tiny as it is it contains the essential centers for the consummation of vital bodily needs, such as hunger, thirst and sex. Information regarding imbalances is fed into the hypothalamus through a number of channels: (1) blood borne factors such as chemicals and hormones; (2) excitatory and inhibitory impulses via fiber tracts (medial forebrain bundle) from the neocortex, limbic system and reticular system; and (3) stimuli from peripheral sensory receptors. Reactions are registered by the hypothalamus through the endocrine and autonomic nervous systems which come under its domain; the former through its connections with the anterior pituitary gland, the latter through centers in its posterolateral part which govern the sympathetic nervous system (provoking the adrenal medulla to pour out epinephrine [adrenalin]) and in its anterior part which stimulates the parasympathic nervous system (producing cholinergic reactions through such releases as the neurohormone acetylcholine). The consequence of these autonomic reverberations is that the hypothalamus can when needs demand such reactions speed up or slow the heart rate, increase or decrease blood pressure, quicken or relax respiration, contract or dilate blood vessels, augment the blood sugar, activate the sweat glands, change the size of the pupils, maintain constant temperature and influence the activities of practically every organ. Excited by stimuli from the external and internal environment, and acting under the dominance of the cerebral cortex which tempers biological drives with past experience and present motivations, the hypothalamus mobilizes the resources of the body for activities that are conducive to the satisfaction of tissue requirements, or for defensive fight and flight reactions. Some consider it a power source for the nervous system (Morgan, 1959) while others believe that it is the principal agency responsible for mood disorders, such as endogenous depressions (Gelhorn, 1963).

Sleeping and dreaming. In recent years sleep and dreaming have occupied the attention of neurophysiologists and other observers (Snyder, 1963; Aserinsky and Kleitman, 1953, 1955; Dement, 1962; Jouvet, 1962; Wolpert and Trosman, 1958). Sleep is a phenomenon found in the lowest forms of life and in the fetuses of higher forms. In man the activated midbrain reticular formation terminates, while its inactivation promotes sleep. Stimuli during sleep are relayed from the reticular formation to the neocortex where they are processed and assayed in terms of their danger or anxiety potentials. Any stimulus interpreted as a threat will excite the neocortex to relay impulses to the reticular formation which in turn will bring about consciousness. Sleep promotes decreased respiration, lowered blood pressure, diminished pulse rate, relaxed muscle tone and peripheral vasodilation, leading to a resting of physical systems.

Dreaming is an essential biological phenomenon that occurs during one of the phases of sleep. The physiological correlate of this phase is a scanning state with rapid eye movements (REMS) accompanied by low voltage electroencephalographic activity. The psychological correlate is hallucinatory dream experience. The REM state is very much different from that of the rest of sleep and apparently serves an important function in all of the higher animal species. Speculation as to the exact function of dreaming in man ranges from ideas that dreaming is a homeostatic device to keep central nervous activity in balance, to formulations regarding its anxiety-binding and goal-directed nature. Dreaming, which occurs three to four times nightly on the average, appears to serve a synthesizing and restorative purpose, preserving the emotional balance. The symbolic composition of dreams is recruited from recent and remote memories. A ruminative reprocessing of the day's residues occurs, fused with past memories, with the formation of symbols that express wish fulfillment, tension alleviation, the presence of inner conflict and of defenses against conflict.

Neurophysiological rationale for the somatic therapies. A number of therapies have been developed empirically for which a neurophysiological rationale is provided. These include drug therapy which attempts to influence specific brain areas through introduction into the body of psychoactive substances. Included also are electroconvulsive and electronarcotic therapy which apparently achieve their effects by changes in the autonomic nervous system during the coma that accompanies and follows treatment (Patterson, 1963). Some authorities believe that depression is resolved and other beneficial consequences scored through stimulation of the sympathetic centers in the posterior hypothalamus (Gelhorn et al., 1963). Others contend that the convulsive state is associated with alterations of cholinergic mechanisms resulting in increased intercellular acetylcholine levels. Irrespective of the mechanisms involved, electrical treatments bring about a profound physiological response, unbalancing the existing equilibrium, stimulating a stress reaction and setting into motion hypothalamic-pituitary mechanisms that whip up the defensive instrumentalities of the body. Acting on the premise that certain mental conditions were accompanied by "fixed arrangements of cellular connections that exist in the brain," Moniz (1936) instituted surgical operations which were aimed at severing the defective area from the rest of the brain. Unfortunately the original operations were so extensive that social adaptation was interfered with. Later operative procedures have been developed which restrict the cutting to small areas, excising portions of the frontal cortex (topectomy) or severing selected parts of the thalmo-frontal radiation (lobotomy. Chemicals and electrical current are also employed to coagulate and destroy the areas under attack. It is probable that these radical procedures interfere with connections to zones of the brain that control feeling and emotion, and that the patient is merely no longer concerned about his abnormal thoughts and ideas and hence makes a better adjustment to them (Freeman and Watts, 1939). Intractable pain, psychotic excitement, incessant obsessional tendencies with exaggerated and persistent anxiety which does not yield to psychotherapy, drug therapy and electroconvulsive therapy have been approached through these surgical techniques with reported favorable results.

II

Biochemical Interactions;
Neuropharmacology,
Psychopharmacology

IF WE WERE TO REDUCE EMOTIONS TO THEIR ELEMENTAL UNITS, we would ultimately impute biochemical reactions. These processes, infinitely complex, and to a large extent still obscure, manipulate the energy resources of the body as well as mediate mood and tension. Through biochemical operations the physiological and psychological equilibrium is maintained. Biochemical disturbances may ultimately disrupt adjustment on all levels. Investigations in the field of biochemistry have proven fruitful not only in understanding the functional mechanics of organ systems and the physical nature of emotions, but also, through the employment of chemical substances (psychoactive drugs) introduced from the outside, in controlling certain aspects of behavior. A startling prediction is that we may some day chemically be able to control and even to modify the human personality (Bello, 1957).

The biochemical interactions which govern brain operations are extremely complex and at our present stage of knowledge not completely understood. However certain broad outlines are clear which permit the following assumptions:

(1) The physiological transactions of the body, including the brain and nervous system, are regulated by intricate biochemical reactions.

(2) Complex chemical substances are constantly being manufactured by enzymes and made available to the tissues for normal metabolic functions.

(3) Deficiencies or surpluses of essential chemical materials may register themselves in pathological functioning of the areas and tracts which are dependent on these elements for proper metabolism.

15

(4) Defective enzymes, released by DNA sources which are deficient because of heredity or altered by disease, will produce vitiated chemical materials. These either fail to supply the systems with essential substances, or act as toxins distorting the operations of the systems for which they have an affinity.

(5) The effect of inadequate, excessive or defective chemical materials may be neutralized or overcome by certain drugs which are increasingly being elaborated and refined. As a consequence we may anticipate more and more pharmacological control of certain aspects of behavior including pathological thinking, feeling and behaving.

Regulation of brain metabolism; biochemistry of depression. How our knowledge of brain metabolism helps in the understanding and management of certain mental disorders may be explicated by biochemical studies of depression. Abundantly present in areas of the brain that are most involved in emotional reactions (recticular, limbic and hypothalamic systems) are two neurohormones: serotonin, which is an indoleamine, and norepinephrine, which is a catecholamine by structure. These substances are stored in body depots in an inactive form, then liberated by enzymes when the need for them comes about. When they have served their purpose, neurohormones are destroyed by other enzymes, such as mono-amine-oxidase (MAO). The regulation site for the production of serotonin is believed by some to be the anterior hypothalamus which is associated with the parasympathic (cholinergic) nervous system. The site for stimulation of norepinephrine (noradrenaline) is presumed to be the posterior hypothalamus which is related to sympathetic (adrenergic) nervous system stimulation. These two systems—the parasympathetic and sympathetic divisions of the autonomic nervous system—are mutually antagonistic and maintain a constant balance in the body. Overactivity of either system, and the ensuing underactivity of the opposing system, register themselves on brain functioning. Thus exaggerated sympathetic activity is apt to induce excessive tension, anxiety and even psychic disorganization. Increased parasympathetic activity leads to tranquilization, and, if parasympathetic stimulation is pathologically intensified, to an abnormal slowing down of body activities, even to the point of depression. What maintains the proper parasympathetic-sympathetic equilibrium is an appropriate (not overabundant) supply of serotonin and norepinephrine. One of the functions of serotonin and norepinephrine is to inhibit excessive parasympathetic stimulation. Where sufficient quantities of these chemicals are not present, parasympathetic activity may get out of hand. This is believed by some to be what happens in depressive states. Excessive serotin and sympathin (derived from norepinephrine) will, on the other hand, exert too great an inhibition on parasympathetic transmission with a corresponding increase of sympathetic activity, leading to excitable emotional reactions.

It is impossible to understand how neurohormones and other chemicals which influence brain activity operate without considering the performances of the synapses. Synapses govern many intricate nerve reactions. When a parasympathetic nerve is stimulated, the chemical, acetylcholine, is released along the fiber and nerve endings at the synapse (end buttons of presynaptic axons) from where it is carried by blood or tissue fluids to the adjacent receptor sites (postsynaptic cell) fostering the transmission of the nerve impulse. However certain "blocking agents" by combining chemically with the receptor site can prevent acetylcholine from affiliating itself with the adjacent receptor site and hence from transmitting an impulse. When a sympathetic nerve is stimulated, norepinephrine and its methylated derivative, epinephrine (adrenaline) are released, large quantities of the latter substance being liberated from the adrenal medulla to circulate freely in the bloodstream. These substances (norepinephrine and epinephrine) are believed to combine into the chemical, sympathin, which apparently acts both as a nerve transmitter for peripheral sympathetic nerves and, at the synapses, serves to inhibit cholinergic (parasympathetic) transmission. Various chemicals are capable of attaching themselves to receptor sites acting to block nerve transmission. A number of such materials have been discovered in recent years which, when introduced into the body, have an affinity for either parasympathetic or sympathetic synapses or both. New blocking agents are constantly being evolved which, by their hampering effect on post-ganglionic sympathetic neural outflow (debrisoquin sulfate, for example), lower the blood pressure and hence are employed in hypertension. One of the actions of the phenothiazine drug, chlorpromazine (Thorazine) is presumed to be an attachment to the receptor sites of parasympathetic nerves, consuming the areas that would ordinarily be occupied by serotonin and sympathin. Displaced in this way, these neurohormones no longer exert an inhibitory effect on cholinergic transmission, fostering greater parasympathetic activity with tranquilization, and, where the reaction is too strong, depression.

In addition to inducing parasympathetic overactivity, deficient quantities of serotonin, some authorities contend, expedite depression through reduction of nutrient cell activity and lowering of the nutrition and oxygen of the nerve cells. This is because serotonin is believed to be a chemical mediator that controls the pulsating action of the cells (oligodendroglia) whose function it is to nourish nerve tissues. Restoring the level of serotonin increases the nutrition of cells. An adequate amount of serotonin is thus apparently essential for normal mental functions, a deficiency or an excess producing mental disorders.

Bound serotonin is present as a potential store, but it is chemically inert and must be released by enzyme action. Free serotonin is rapidly metabolized by the enzyme mono-amine-oxidase. The drug Reserpine acts by releasing serotonin from its stores in large quantities, eventually depleting the level of free serotonin. This has led to the hypothesis that in conditions such as depression, a similar mechanism takes place. To restore the serotonin to a normal level it must either be synthesized in more abundant quantities, new binding sites being formed or old ones restored, or the enzyme that destroys it (mono-amine-oxidase) must be inhibited. The latter action is obtained with certain drugs such as hydrazines (MAO inhibitors like Marsalid). There is evidence also that the catecholamines, especially norepinephrine, are implicated, low concentrations of which encourage depression (Schildkraut, 1965). MAO inhibitors increase the brain concentration of norepinephrine, and tend to neutralize depression.

Since it is hypothesized that depression is a product of excessive parasympathetic stimulation and faulty cell nutrition, a blocking of parasympathetic transmission and a bettering of cell metabolism should restore the proper nutritive and sympathetic-parasympathetic balance, thus resolving depression. A search for chemicals that can effectuate this resulted in the discovery of several different inhibitors of the neurohormone (serotonin and norepinephrine) destroying enzyme, mono-amine-oxidase, that are not as toxic as Marsalid. The use of such inhibitors as tranylcypromine (Parnate), phenelzine (Nardil) and isocarboxid (Marplan) has been clinically effective in reversing certain depressive conditions. Employing the same hypothesis, if we introduce drugs that activate sympathetic transmission to excess, this should also correct depression. Such substances as amphetamine (Benzedrine, Dexedrine, Dexamyl) methylphenidate (Ritalin) and Meratran have to some extent been successful in milder depressive states, probably through their effect on sympathetic activity. Imipramine (Tofranil) and desipramine (Pertofrane, Norpramin) appear also to sensitize adrenergic synapses potentiating the sympathetic action of norepinephrine. Excessive sympathetic stimulation will, of course, sponsor excitement.

Psychoactive drugs. The possession of drugs that depress or excite certain areas of the brain and nervous system, that may induce hallucinations or abolish them, enables the experimental psychiatrist, psychologist or pharmacologist to study brain functions in health and disease at chemical, electrical and behavioral levels. Since drugs exert different effects both electrically and behaviorally on every animal species, experiments on subhuman varieties have only a presumptive applicability to man. Such investigations have nevertheless opened vast areas for the clinical study of psychoactive substances.

By their action on specific areas of the brain, psychoactive drugs influence such provinces as perception, discrimination, conditioning, reasoning, learning, conflict and motor behavior. Drug effects depend on their depressant or stimulant impact on neural masses. Thus the barbiturates depress the neocortex, reticular formation, limbic system and hypothalamus, while stimulating the thalamus. The substituted alkeneodiols (Meprobamate) depress the thalamus and limbic system. The Rauwolfia derivatives (Reserpine) stimulate the reticular formation and limbic system, depress the sympathetic mechanisms of the hypothalamus (at the same time that they activate parasympathetic mechanisms) and deplete the neurohormones (serotonin, norepinephrine). The phenothiazines depress the reticular formation and sympathetic mechanisms of the hypothalamus, stimulate the thalamus and limbic systems and block the neurohormones. Chart I illustrates some of the presumed effects of different drugs.

In studying the reactions of the various brain areas to drugs, and noting the pathological symptoms that are alleviated in their administration, we may ask some pertinent questions. Why, for instance, do phenothiazines relieve psychotic thinking in schizophrenic disorders? It is known that the phenothiazines have an activating effect on the limbic system, particularly the amygdaloid complex. This action apparently breaks up the rhinencephalic chain reaction and isolates the midbrain reticular formation from the limbic system. From this we may assume that the limbic system has something to do with cognitive processes and that regulation of its function is a factor in controlling the morbid thinking that occurs in schizophrenia. Focal sites have been hypothesized through drug effects for such symptoms as anxiety, obsessions, depression, excitement, hallucinations and delusions.

The use of psychoactive drugs to influence such "target symptoms" is still in an experimental stage, although sufficient data has accumulated to indicate that drugs constitute an important, perhaps vital tool in the management of emotionally ill persons. More or less, drugs are employed on an empirical basis, the mechanisms by which they exert their beneficial effects being only partially clear. They are generally divided into tranquilizing, stimulant and psychotomimetic varieties.

Tranquilizers have a calming effect in tension and anxiety, as well as an antipsychotic influence in schizophrenic and organic psychosis, producing what has been referred to as a "chemical lobotomy." Major tranquilizers, such as the neuroleptics (phenothiazines, Rauwolfia derivatives) repress conditioned avoidance behavior and reduce aggressive activities. Minor tranquilizers (meprobamate, chlordiazepoxide, etc.) have an effect on mild to moderate anxiety. Stimulant drugs ("antidepressants," "psychic energizers," "thymoleptics," "psychic activators") reduce depression, increase alertness, and enhance physical and mental activity. Psychotomimetics (mescaline, psilocybin, LSD) act as toxins to nerve tissue inducing "model psychoses." Chart II outlines the therapeutic uses of the more popular drugs.

CHART I
BRAIN FUNCTIONING AND PSYCHOACTIVE DRUGS

BRAIN AREA	FUNCTION	CHEMICAL EFFECT	DRUG
NEOCORTEX	Thinking; Reasoning	Stimulation	Caffein, Amphetamine (1) Methylphenidate (10)
		Depression	Barbiturates (3) Nonbarbiturate Hypnotics (11)
THALAMUS	Integrating Sensation; Transmitting and Modulating Alerting Impulses	Stimulation	Barbiturates (3), Phenothiazines (13)
		Depression	Meprobamate (9)
RETICULAR FORMATION	Alerting; Integrating Emotional Responses to Stimuli	Stimulation	Rauwolfia Derivatives (14) (small doses)
		Depression	Phenothiazines (13) Barbiturates (3) Rauwolfia Derivatives (14) (large doses), Amitriptyline (2) Imipramine (7), Methylphenidate (10), Nonbarbiturate Hypnotics (11)
LIMBIC SYSTEM	Regulating Emotions	Stimulation	Phenothiazines (13), Rauwolfia Derivatives (14)
		Depression	Meprobamate (9), Barbiturates (3) Chlordiazepoxide (4) Diazepam (5) Oxazepam (12), Tybamate (15) Hydroxyzine (6)
HYPOTHALAMUS	Controlling Autonomic and Endocrine Functions	Stimulation	*MAO Inhibitors (hydrazines) (8) Amphetamine (1)
		Depression	Phenothiazines (13) Rauwolfia Derivatives (14) Barbiturates (3)
SYNAPSES	Transmitting Nerve Impulses	Stimulation	Rauwolfia Derivatives (14) Acetylcholine
		Depression	Epinephrine, Amphetamine (1) Mescaline, LSD, Imipramine (7) Amitriptyline (2) Gamma aminobutyric acid
INTERNEURONAL CIRCUITS	Coordinating Neuronal Masses	Depression	Meprobamate (9)
NEUROHORMONAL DEPOTS (serotonin norepinephrine, etc)	Regulating Brain Metabolism	Stimulation	MAO Inhibitors (8) Imipramine (7)
		Depression	Phenothiazines (13) Rauwolfia Derivatives (14) Benzoquinolizenes

* Electroconvulsive Therapy is said to stimulate the posterior hypothalamus (Gelhorn et. al, 1963) (1) Amphetamine (Benzedrine, Dexedrine, etc.); (2) Amitriptyline (Elavil); (3) Barbiturates (Phenobarbital, Pentothal, Seconal, etc.); (4) Chlordiazepoxide (Librium); (5) Diazepam (Valium); (6) Hydroxyzine (Vistaril); (7) Imipramine (Tofranil) Desipramine (Norpramin, Pertofrane); (8) MAO Inhibitors (Nardil, Marplan, Niacin, etc.); (9) Meprobamate (Equinal, Miltown) (10) Methylphenidate (Ritalin); (11) Nonbarbiturate Hypnotics (Doriden, Noludar, etc.); (12) Oxazepam (Serax); (13) Phenothiazines (Thorazine, Stelazine, Mellaril, Trilafon, Permitil, etc.); (14) Rauwolfia Derivatives (Reserpine etc.); (15) Tybamate (Solacen)

Paradoxically, drugs do not affect all persons the same way. Individuals vary in the constitutional sensitivity (elaborateness of neural circuits?) of their nervous systems and in their chemical structure (enzyme systems?). It is to be expected that there will be varying responses to the array of substances that are available in the drug market. This is borne out clinically by the highly selective reactions that all individuals display toward drugs. Thus some persons respond better to Miltown than to Valium, and vice versa. Some cannot tolerate Thorazine, yet do well with Mellaril. Eysenck (1957) has posed the interesting idea that persons with excitatory and inhibitory personality dispositions behave differently with drugs not only in terms of speed of reaction, but in strength of response. The current status of one's metabolism ("law of initial values" Wilder, 1958) also influences how one reacts; thus a drug may have a pronounced effect at one time and a minimal effect at another. One of the most important of intervening variables is the placebo factor; faith in and anticipated reactions to the drug determining the quality of response, even to a suggested action diametrically opposite to the true chemical reaction. Fluctuations in the environment of various kinds also register significantly on drug reactivity.

Model psychoses. Model psychoses are an interesting means of studying the relation between biological systems and behavior. In 1884 Thudichum presented the idea that many kinds of insanity "unquestionably were the external manifestations of the effects upon the brain substances of poisons fermented within the body." Though not identifiable then, Thudichum predicted the eventual discovery of these toxic products and their neutralization by proper antidotes. Modern biochemical studies give some credence to Thudichum's theory. The fact that it is possible to produce symptoms seen in psychoses by ingesting minute quantities of toxic materials, raises the possibility that noxious agents, internally manufactured as a result of disordered metabolism, may similarly be responsible for the psychotic process. Although there is still no uncontrovertible proof of the relationship of biochemical abnormalities and schizophrenia, as Kety (1965) has pointed out, indications of a relationship are too many to dismiss the possibility

CHART II

SYMPTOMATIC USES OF PSYCHOACTIVE DRUGS

DESIRED DRUG EFFECT	DRUG
Enhancing Cortical Activity (facilitating alertness and thinking).	Amphetamine (Benzedrine, Dexedrine, Dexamyl) Methylphenidate (Ritalin) Caffeine
Diminishing Excessive Cortical Activity (producing calming and sedation).	Barbiturates (Phenobarbital) Nonbarbiturate hypnotics (Doriden) Bromides (Triple Bromides)
Elevating Mood (overcoming depression).	Amphetamine (Benzedrine, Dexedrine, Dexamyl) Methylphenidate (Ritalin) Mono-amino-oxidase Inhibitors (Nardil, Parnate, Marplan) Amitriptyline (Elavil) Imipramine (Tofranil) Desipramine (Pertofrane, Norpramin)
Eliminating Apathy (especially in borderline or schizophrenic states).	Phenothiazines with a piperidine or piperazine ring on side chain (Mellaril, Stelazine, Trilafon)
Inhibiting Excitement, Confusion, Tension and Anxiety (especially in schizophrenic and manic states).	Phenothiazines (Thorazine, Mellaril)
Restoring Mental Integration (controlling hallucinations and delusions).	Phenothiazines (Thorazine, Mellaril, Stelazine, Permitil, Trilafon, etc.) Rauwolfia Derivatives (Reserpine)
Producing "Model Psychoses" (for abreactions and hypermnesia).	LSD, Mescaline, Psilocybin

that a schizophrenic outbreak is supported by biochemical disturbances.

Many attempts have been made to set up experimentally induced psychoses through injection or ingestion of exogenous toxins. While such model psychoses have permitted some generalizations regarding organic psychoses (Hoch, 1959), endeavors to derive valid inferences regarding the mechanisms of schizophrenia have not been possible (Freedman, 1960; Grinker, 1963; Kety, 1965). Nonetheless, drug induced psychoses have considerable value as an experimental means of studying certain psychological functions. Among the most commonly employed psychotomimetics are psilocybin, mescaline and LSD.

Intravenous injection of mescaline will produce perceptual distortions and alterations of the body image, accompanied by vivid symbolizations, infantile wish-fulfilling fantasies, auditory and visual hallucinations, distortions of proprioceptive sensation, development of paranoidal, grandiose or hypochondriacal ideas, depersonalization, flight of ideas, ambivalence and negativism that seem akin to phenomena in schizophrenia. Though aware of the experimental situation, the individual lacks insight into the ideas that he expresses.

D-lysergic acid diethylamide (LSD-25) is a synthetic amide belonging to the ergot family which was discovered by the Swiss chemist, Albert Hofmann, in 1947. Administered even in small quantities it produces a psychotic reaction analogous to that of an organic psychosis as well as schizophrenia. Approximately half an hour following oral administration of the drug (1-2 micrograms per kilogram of body weight) the individual begins to exhibit symptoms which reach their peak in from two to three hours and then slowly decline so that there is a gradual return to the original state after six hours or so. LSD influences the vegetative and especially sympathetic nervous system, producing dizziness, nausea, headache, malaise, palpitations, sweating, dilated pupils, diuresis, ataxia, dysarthric speech, anxiety along with euphoria, silliness and impulsive laughter. Administered to borderline and schizophrenic patients, LSD exaggerates their thinking disorder and intensifies the emotional disturbance. Some patients respond with relaxation, drowsiness and euphoria; others with panic, and still others with depression and retardation.

Irrespective of mental status, changes are registered in spatial orientation, and visual and somesthetic perceptions are common, especially when the subject is lying down in a darkened room. Distances shift from being greater and then lesser, walls close in or pulsate, objects appear to disintegrate. Illusions and hallucinations of lights, brilliant colors, geometric patterns and objects burst into the attentive field, to which the individual may react as if they are real. Synesthesia (fusion of sensations) may occur. Thus a loud sound may cause a visual hallucination of color to appear. Numbness and paresthesia are present. Depersonalization and alterations in body image also develop, the individual becoming unable to differentiate himself from persons and objects around him. The time sense is markedly distorted; minutes may seem like hours or days. Perceptual disturbances may be extended to persons in the environment from whom the subject usually feels detached and upon whom various distorted feelings may be projected. Perceptual impairments involve the self and environment and the confusion of fantasy and reality are common. Some neurophysiological research has been done on the effect of LSD on perception. Purpura (1956) has shown that LSD produces a stimulation of some systems, such as the optical system (by facilitating axosomatic synaptic activity) while inhibiting transmission along pathways within the cortex, thus preventing the cortex from integrating perceptual stimuli. This alteration in the transmission and integration of messages has a disturbing effect on cognition.

Vicissitudes in the thinking process occur with LSD which take the form of an undirected, dreamlike quality fused with brilliant, luminous and bizarre imagery difficult to describe in the language of reality. Thinking, reasoning, problem solving, memory and association are impaired (Jarvik et al., 1955). In some instances pathways are opened to remote memories, even to those in infancy. A dissolution of boundaries between autonomous and conflictual areas of the ego has been suggested (Weintraub et al., 1959). Impaired conduction in association pathways of the cortex along with excitation of subcortical centers (limbic system) are said to account for some of the thinking disturbances (Bridger, 1960; Klee, 1963).

Not all of the phenomena accompanying LSD are indicative of deteriorated functioning. In inhibited and detached individuals, for example, the abreactive experience may open the door to a more fluid, freer and more imaginative expression of feeling and thinking, providing the individual with a wondrous and spectacular demonstration of his perceptual and cognitive potentials. Such release from inhibition may prove to be liberating, at least temporarily, for some individuals, although beneficial effects must be judged in the context of the potentially harmful influence that LSD can have for individuals whose hold on reality is at best tenuous.

Experimental studies with LSD are indicative of the contemporary efforts that are being made to correlate neurophysiological, biochemical and psychological processes which have both heuristic and practical value. There are some investigators who believe that the administration of drugs such as mescaline and LSD is justified as an adjunct in psychotherapy to investigate personality structure, since ego defenses become weakened and the patient is better able to reveal himself. In the course of overcoming resistance, painful and repressed emotions are brought to the fore, unconscious material being liberated. Abramson (1955) contends that the anxiety experience intensifies the relationship with the therapist during the drug induced state, and that this has a marked influence on the helping process. Instead of employing the large doses to induce an experimental psychosis, Abramson recommends small quantities (25 to 50 units). Denber (1955) contends that mescaline also has a therapeutic effect in freeing thoughts and emotions associated with past events. According to Hoch (1959) LSD and mescaline facilitate psychotherapy in much the same way as substances like sodium amytal, benzedrine and carbon dioxide. The effects, however, cannot be predicted. Some patients under the influence of mescaline and LSD achieve benefit; most do not. How the drug is administered and the activities of the therapist influence the results. A number of patients refuse later to participate in psychotherapy because the experiences that they encounter during the period of drug intoxication are so upsetting. For some reason alcoholics appear to respond better than other patients.

Schizophrenia. The ability of LSD, mescaline and related drugs to induce psychotic states has given rise to the hypothesis that certain toxic chemicals may act similarly as psychotic producing substances. Most of the experimental work has centered around schizophrenia. Implicated have been faulty amino acids, which, circulating in the blood and influencing the brain, are said to resemble mescaline and LSD in their effect. Particularly accused have been the indoles, the catechols and gamma-amino-butyric acid. Since there is some evidence that psychic changes may be brought about in normal persons by altering the metabolism of serotonin, this neurohormone has been inculpated by a number of observers as a principal offender in schizophrenia. Another hypothesis is that schizophrenia is a product of abnormal derivatives of epinephrine, such as adrenochrome or adrenolutin, produced by an enzymic, possibly genetic defect, which results in a toxic concentration of such materials in the face of stress. Some authorities believe that the faulty oxidation of epinephrine is produced by ceruloplasmin or a variant of ceruloplasmin. Epinephrine, released by stress, is thus not properly dissipated and becomes hallucinogenic. Other suspected substances include taraxein and excessive methylated derivatives of normal metabolities. All of the experimental studies are highly suggestive of disturbed metabolism as one variable in the complex picture of schizophrenia, although to date the specific mechanisms and substances responsible are not known.

III

Genetics, Behavior Genetics
and Ethology

It is natural to asssume that genetic factors, which govern the integrity of enzyme and hormone sources, must play some role in adaptation, since if through heredity certain body chemicals are deficient, the reactions they mediate will also be inadequate in meeting adaptive needs. By interfering with proper metabolic processes within the brain, or selected areas of the brain, genetic components may thus potentially sponsor or support emotional disturbance or render the individual more susceptible to psychological deterioration (Grinker, 1964).

The function of the genes is to fix the specificity of proteins within the cell. Genes (of which there are approximately 10,000) are strung like beads on filaments of the chromosomes. Each gene is a complex aggregate of nucleotides (desoxyribonucleic acid or "DNA") whose molecular weight ranges from two to two million. Paired purine and pyrimidine bases imbedded in a linear polymer in various sequential configurations make up a code that contains essential genetic information. Suspended in twin hellical strands, DNA serves as a template in which nucleotides identical with the model are elaborated for the construction of a complementary chain whenever replication of the cell is in order, or when specific needs of the cell dictate the manufacture of protein materials for: (1) the intrinsic cellular structure; (2) enzymes to govern the internal cellular metabolism; and (3) hormones for external cellular use. The instrumentality that DNA employs for the latter three purposes is RNA (ribonucleic acid) various forms of which are also fashioned from its template. Errors in the construction of a chain alter the information and result in genetic modifications. These changes become fixed hereditary character-

28

istics and make for variations in those structures and functions which fall under the aegis of the implicated genes.

An example, is sickle cell disease, which, caused by a change at a single gene locus, leads to a specific alteration in the amino acid sequence of the globin molecule, resulting in abnormal homoglobin. In phenylketonuria, those children who inherit two abnormal genes, one from each parent, will possess no phenyl-alanine hydroxylase, the enzyme that changes phenylalanine to tyrosine. The consequence of this error in metabolism is a form of mental retardation. Similarly genetic metabolic defects exist in galactosemia, fibrocystic disease of the pancreas, glycogen storage disease, blood glutathione instability, and other physical abnormal-ities that exert an indirect impact on behavior. Chromosomal diseases of a hereditary nature have also been discovered which have an influence on higher level functions. The normal chromo-somal number in man is forty-six. In Mongolian idiocy there is an additional small chromosome which produces a developmental imbalance. Abnormal chromosome numbers also are present in gonadal agenesis (Turner's syndrome) and in testicular dysgenesis (Klinefelter's syndrome). Individuals with certain hereditary abnormalities will react adversely to specific drugs, as toward barbiturates in the hereditary hepatic porphyria, and toward anesthetics in familial dysautonomia.

Biochemical genetic factors manifest themselves also by enzymic overproduction and excessive accumulation of some necessary sub-strate. It has been possible to eliminate unused substrate by drugs as in gout, or to prevent its amassment as by eliminating phenyl-alanine from the diet where there is a predisposition to phenyl-ketonuria. In the latter case, if recognized early enough, mental retardation can be prevented.

Since most of the known inherited ailments exhibit a recessive pattern of inheritance, such diseases as phenylketonuria could be wiped out by preventing the mating of two carriers. This has raised the possibility of genetic counseling both to advise couples who are carriers of known hereditary diseases who contemplate marriage, and to counsel those who have already married.

Behavior genetics. Through complex biochemical reactions, the genes determine the morphological characteristics of the individual. They are responsible, too, for a number of behavioral attributes, although these are more difficult to define in man than in lower animals. Investigation of the activities of lower animals reveals that many basic constellations, such as courting, mating, fighting and escape patterns, are genetically determined. Mutations developing in a species evidence subtle behavioral features that differ distinctively from those of the parent strain, the variant characteristics being passed on by the substrains to their offspring (Keeler and King, 1942; Denenberg et al., 1963). Extensive animal research on strain differences and the effects of selection indicate that there are striking genetically based distinctions in behavior among groupings of animals of even the same strain (King and Mavromatis, 1956; King and Eleftheriou, 1959; Schaefer, 1959; Royce and Covington, 1960; Ginsburg, 1960), although some of these variations are produced by divergencies in emotional, motivational and peripheral processes rather than by genetic dissimilarities in central processes (Scott, 1963). The assumptions that we may draw from these experiments are that strains of human beings probaby also exist who respond variantly to training, learning and stress; that interaction of genotype and environment are constant; and that environmental forces will have diverse effects upon the same genetic backgrounds.

Experimental selective breeding cannot, of course, be practiced with humans as it can with animals, nor can the conditions of rearing be controlled. Accordingly we must rely on clinical observations from which we may make inferences. Since gene-environmental variations are continuous, it is difficult to assign to any trait specific genetic qualities, for instance in relation to intelligence. Thus children of defective parents who show a low I.Q. may reflect the restricted intelligence of the parental models, and/or may actually be impaired because of hereditary factors. However we do know that intelligence test performances show correlations between parents and children of .5, far above the correlations from .07 to .24 between foster parents and children (Jones, 1965). Correlations between identical twins range around .9, while those of fraternal twins score around .6, even when the twins are reared apart (Newman et al., 1937). These studies would seem to indicate that intelligence possesses high hereditary properties. On the other hand, personality tests do not show correlations suggestive of hereditary determinants.

That sensitivity and activity potentials are inherited is probable from both animal studies and human observation. Highly sensitive and malleable nervous systems respond intensely to stimuli and activate coping mechanisms, such as avoidance patterns, that may act as foci for neurotic syndromes. Disintegrative tendencies in the face of stress may, as has already been indicated, be the product of genetic deficiencies in enzyme systems that fail to dispose of the end products of stress, or that promote the synthesis of abnormal chemicals sponsoring toxic reactions.

Statistical studies yield some clues regarding genetic factors in mental illness. The charting of the rates of manic-depressive psychoses among relatives of affected persons indicate higher correlations than among relatives of nonaffected persons. This, of course, could suggest an environmental as well as hereditary influence. However among identical twins the expectencies are almost five times greater than among fraternal twins. There are indications too that some forms of schizophrenia are genetically determined (Kallman, 1962), while others seem to be principally related to environmental factors. Mental retardation similarly breaks down into: (1) genetic varieties—for instance, mongolism, phenylketonuric oligophrenia, and some types of cretinism; and (2) environmental varieties, like those associated with birth trauma.

Ethological approaches. The field of ethology is concerned with the comparative investigation of behavior and the examination of homologous motor patterns among the different species. Its findings are potentially of value to those interested in problems of human adaptation (Kramer, 1965; Lorenz, 1937, 1948; Tinbergen, 1951, 1963; Wheeler, 1903, 1910; Heinroth, 1910; Whitman, 1919). As a consequence of ethological research, the evidence is overwhelming that innately arranged assemblies of neurons exist in all animals including man, which, registered indelibly within the neural system during the course of evolution, subserve important adaptive aims, particularly in relation to self and species preservation. They are responsible for neuromuscular coordinations that promote feeding, mating, attack and flight activities. These patterns are liberated by specific stimuli in the environment ("releasers"), the threshold of response to the stimuli being dependent on the intensity of need (hunger, fear, etc.) within the organism as well as the strength of stimulus. Innate patterns may lead to interaction in the direction of complex behavioral and social activities.

Direct observation of animals in their natural habit, the rearing of animals in isolation, and the crossbreeding of related species have brought out the following facts:

(1) Species specific behavioral features may be identified among nonvertebrates and vertebrates in the form of fixed motor patterns which are inherited and not learned, and which are progressively released during successive epochs of maturation.

(2) Distinctive for each species are stereotyped neuromuscular units which control feeding, respiratory and locomotor responses, as well as more complex operations, such as fighting rituals for territory, and courtship, mating and parental patterns.

(3) New combinations of patterns may be observed in hybrids, while some older innate traits that were present in the parents may be suppressed through crossbreeding.

(4) Basic needs (drives) such as hunger, sex, etc., activated by tissue demands and hormones, are satisfied through the exercise of specific unlearned hereditary patterns.

(5) In higher animals, certain brain areas are intimately involved in innate reactions, for instance the hypothalamus and limbic system in man.

(6) Selective stimuli ("releasers") such as scents, colors, sounds and movements will bring need-gratifying neuromuscular coordinations into play. Patterns remain inhibited until the "innate releasing mechanism," an unconditioned response, is stimulated. For example, a tick may remain immobile for months or years on a leaf until the butyric acid emanating from the body of an animal passing underneath releases coordinations in the tick which result in its dropping on the animal and sinking its feeding apparatus into the animal's skin.

(7) The threshold of response is affected by the internal physiological state, an inversely proportionate relationship existing between the strength of the releasing stimulus and the inten-

sity of inner need. A powerful stimulus can activate a response even though the inner physiological need is low; a strong inner need may touch off a reaction with the barest minimum of stimulus. Thus, in the presence of intense sexual desire, a provocative thought or sound can immediately arouse the sexual mechanism in man. The absence of such inner excitation will require powerful external or phantasy stimulation for an equivalent reaction.

(8) Two sets of motor patterns simultaneously stimulated, which inhibit each other, as for instance, aggressive and escape behavior, will result in conflict and may promote *displacement* activity in the form of a third pattern.

(9) Motor reactions may not be pursued to the completion of an act; they may be attenuated in the form of rituals, functioning as expressive signals to other animals as an intention to act. Thus the baring of teeth and growling may become a releaser of a retreat pattern in another animal who interprets the signal as a symbolic attack. Many ritualized maneuvers are established in the process of natural selection. Crying in man is conceived of by some authorities as a parental-invoking ritual derived from the scream; grief, an inhibited scream, is also a form of communication for help from a parental agency.

(10) While fixed motor patterns essential to the economy and survival of the organism are demonstrable in all animals, including man, the mechanism of their formation still remains to be solved. The consistent orderly arrangement of sensorimotor neurons that promote complex adaptive activities involves embryological, cytological and physicochemical phenomena that undoubtedly will become more transparent with continuing research.

Psychoanalysis shares with ethology a common concern with the hereditary nature of behavioral patterns and the dynamic interaction of these patterns with external (ecological) influences. In man this admixture leads to organization of the character structure. The biological origin of social structure is less positively accepted although this has been posited by Freudian psychoanalysts as well as by non-analysts like Briffault (1959). Presented as evidence for the physiological basis of social behavior are studies among apes (Yerkes, 1929), baboons (Zuckerman, 1932), howler monkeys (Carpenter, 1934) and Japanese macaques (Kawamura, 1959; Itani, 1959). Contended is the fact that social behavior involves groups of fixed motor patterns and their releasing stimuli (releasers) which are responsible for activities from simple rituals to complex social organizations.

IV

The Conditioning of Neural Circuits

ALL LIVING THINGS ARE CONSTANTLY SEARCHING THE ENVIRON-
ment for opportunities to feed and reproduce. Man is no excep-
tion. The mechanisms through which his self and species preservation activities operate are focused, as we have seen, in highly
sensitive, chemically regulated groups of cells in the hypothalamus
and limbic systems. One group of cells becomes activated when the
glucose level of the body falls below a certain point, stimulating
cortical, subcortical and autonomic neuromuscular coordinations
to obtain, digest and distribute food. When the glucose concentration rises, the food regulating cells become quiescent and the
mechanisms they stimulate cease. Another group of cells, which
becomes especially excitable during puberty, administers the drive
for sex and is influenced by the amassment of a number of polariz-
able amines, such as epinephrine, norepinephrine, acetylcholine,
histamine, 5-hydroxtryptamine, in addition to other chemicals.
When the cumulation reaches a surplus, the cells discharge impulses throughout the nervous system energizing various sensory,
motor and autonomic feedback mechanisms. Tension mounts,
and when it reaches a pitch there is a discharge in orgasm, resulting in a reduction of the concentration of amines and chemicals
in the cells which become quiescent again. Cellular masses also
govern other fixed motor patterns in relation to rageful-attack
and fearful-flight activities.

Genetically determined pathways then provide the initial routes
for impulses from these hypothalamic and limbic system regulators
and are designed, as a product of evolution, to bring about responses from the environment, propitiating the needs inspired by
the activated groups of cells. For instance, hunger in the neonate
promotes inherited autonomic respiratory and other muscular
coordinations in the form of thrashing about and screaming. This

invokes the mother to hold the infant close to her body, to feed and comfort him. Soon the mother, her presence and ministrations, become affiliated in the infant's developing mind, with the satisfaction of the hunger response. Sexual coordinations are less apparent at birth, but are probably present in an undifferentiated form during the first years of life, appearing more obviously during puberty. The extensive cultural stimuli to which the sexual response becomes related makes for a highly complex repertoire of releasing mechanisms that become capable of stimulating the sex cells. The groupings of cells controlling rage and fear promote various coordinations that become more and more highly diversified with experience.

Closely associated with these cellular aggregates are two highly sensitive clusters of neurons, which will be dealt with later, that produce in their stimulation feelings of either pleasure or pain. For instance, discomfort and pain are consequent to an overwhelming conflux of charges within the cells that administer feeding and sex; pleasure results when the cells lose their charge. In this way motivation is provided for the pursuit of drives that satisfy basic cellular needs as well as other promptings that become associatively linked to the pleasure–pain centers. The desire for pleasure and the avoidance of pain come to constitute the fuel of human incentive. Their indulgence will exploit networks of approach and avoidance developed in the nexus of experience.

Classical and Operant Conditioning. The binding together of the perceptual organs, sensory receptors, neocortex, subcortical brain areas, spinal cord, autonomic nervous system, efferent nerves, glands and muscles into unified assemblies that fulfill goal directed needs is accomplished through the process of conditioning. By means of conditioning, thoughts and verbal symbols become capable of evoking physiological responses and of initiating purposeful activities.

It is to the credit of Ivan Pavlov that the experimental foundation of conditioning was established. Interested in determining the nature of higher central nervous functions, Pavlov discovered the conditioned reflex in 1901 which he employed as an investigative tool. With Sechenov, who developed a materialistic approach to the physiology of the nervous system, Pavlov expanded the viewpoint that all mental processes, including consciousness, were aspects of organic brain functioning, and that the external material world, which is independent of consciousness, determined what exists in consciousness. This viewpoint, including the contention that man's subjective mind could be accounted for in purely physiological terms, and examined by scientific experimental methods, has separated Pavlov's work from that of William James and Sigmund Freud whose ideas, developed in the same era as those of Pavlov, took the form of more speculative theories about impalpable instinctual processes and elusive psychological functioning.

Pavlov demonstrated that a neutral stimulus (conditioned stimulus, "CS") paired with a stimulus (unconditioned stimulus "US") that produces an unlearned (innate) response (unconditioned response, "UR") will, after a number of pairings, elicit the same response (conditioned response, "CR"). Once a conditioned response is constituted, "second order" conditioning can be established by pairing a new neutral stimulus with the conditioned stimulus. Pavlov believed that positive conditioned reflexes were related to the central process of "excitation," while negative conditioned reflexes were associated with the central process of "inhibition." Generalization of both conditioned stimuli and responses occurred, but reinforcements served to make them more specific. Individual differences in conditioning were due to constitutional variations in the excitatory-inhibitory endowment, and in the strength and mobility of responsivity.

In Pavlovian descriptions of personality typology, the relationship of two "signal systems" operative in man played an important part. The "first signal system" was the primary or concrete system, which was supplemented by the "second signal system" in which words and abstractions took the place of direct stimuli. The systems could be balanced ("intermediate" personality type), weighted in the direction of the primary system ("artistic type") or in the direction of the secondary system ("thinking type"). These personality types were disposed toward different syndromes. Essentially, disturbances were products of difficulties within and across the two signal systems produced by forces interfering with the complex biosocial adjustment required of man.

While Pavlov's ideas regarding conditioning have acted as the basis for modern learning theory, his notions about personality structure and functioning have not had a universal appeal. A number of practical applications of Pavlovian hypotheses have been made, for instance his concept of "protective inhibition" has been utilized in sleep therapy to provide a means for the recovery of "exhausted cortical cells." Students of Pavlov have extended his researches widely and have substantiated many of his findings by the techniques of electrophysiology and histochemistry. The effect of drugs on conditioning has also been studied and the modification of various types of psychopathology through conditioning procedures have been attempted, acting as a basis for present-day "behavior therapy."

Pavlovian theorists are convinced that all pathology of higher nervous activity involves the formation of pathological conditioned connections which nurture pathological functional reactions. Eventually these become stabilized and are set into motion by conditioned stimuli in the environment. What accounts for the involvement of the selected areas of the brain is also of interest in understanding conditioned reflex connections. It is probable that all stimuli at first excite the brain as a whole. However certain regions are more sensitive than others, being in a functional state of subliminal excitement. These regions will be most susceptible to low increments of stimulation and will most readily offer themselves for the establishment of conditioning connections.

Present-day neurophysiologists, employing many of the concepts of Pavlov, have demonstrated the vital role played by subcortical mechanisms in the conditioning process (Magoun, 1960). For example, blocking of the alpha rhythm of the occipital area of the brain occurs when a subject is exposed to visual stimulation. If an auditory stimulus is adventitiously paired with the visual stimulus, it will become the conditioned stimulus to set off the conditioned responses of blocked alpha rhythm, at first over wide areas of the cortex, including the midbrain reticular formation, then in the occipital area exclusively. Initial generalization of the response is believed to be mediated by the reticular formation, while closure in conditional learning and focal localization involves the projecting thalamic nuclei (thalamo-cortical projections). Anokhin has shown in many experiments that by their numerous and diverse influences on the cerbral cortex through various pathways, the subcortical structures constantly participate in conditioned reflex formation, determining the direction of cerebral cortex selectivity. Subcortical influences on cortical activity cannot be minimized. Correspondingly, according to Anokhin, nearly every cortical neuron has on its body and dendrites numerous synaptic contacts making it potentially available to all of the ascending influences.

"Protective inhibition" is generally accepted as of utmost importance in the integrative activity of the central nervous system. But where in the conditioned reflex the inhibitory process takes place is disputed. In the nerve cells of the conditioned brain foci? In the internuclial neurones? In special inhibitory structures which are apart from excitatory areas in the cortex? Irrespective of locus, cortical inhibition is a functional tenet in Pavlovian theory. Important in understanding how some neurotic patterns originate and continue to perpetuate themselves are certain experiments described by Kupalov in which delayed conditioned reflexes result in consistent abnormal irradiations of inhibition that spread extensively over various functions unrelated to the original conditioning. Such inhibitions initiated by the cerebral cortex, spread expansively over the cortex and subcortex, and may persist for years.

The central processes of excitation and inhibition, according to modern Pavlovians, underlie all higher activities of the central nervous system. The balance of these two processes, related to the constitutional make-up of the individual, predispose him to either basic excitatory or inhibitory potentials of an enduring nature. Postulated also is a reactive inhibition of nerve tissue to stimulation which supplements the basic inhibitory tendencies. Individuals with predominantly inhibitory reactivity are said to form conditioned responses less easily and to extinguish them more readily than those with an excitatory disposition. Eysenck (1957, 1960b) has broadened this hypothesis by insisting that the excitatory-inhibitory substratum underlies personality types, particularly influencing tendencies toward introversion or extroversion. Thus excitatory nervous systems are disposed to introversive patterns and will more readily develop dysthymic reactions like anxiety. Inhibitory systems will lean toward extroverted behavior and hysteric-psychopathic symptoms. Excitatory and inhibitory predispositions of nerve tissue may also, according to Eysenck, explain the varying reactions to drugs.

Psychopathology, through the Pavlovian lens, is viewed as a disturbance between the two signal systems which can be produced by many agencies such as environmental trauma, organic disease, fatigue, drugs or toxic states. Psychoses, like the schizophrenias, are considered by Pavlovian theorists to be based on pathological excitations of connections of the second signal system, with a derangement of their interrelations and their dominance over the first signal system. A measurement of bioelectric potentials of the cerebral cortex indicates that, as a result of consistent inert excitation, there develops in the cells of the cerebral cortex a widespread exhaustion leading to "protective inhibition" which spreads to individual signal systems or analyzers. A developing chain reaction results in an increasing magnification of the pathogenic links. As one observes the bioelectric mozaic in the chlorpromazine therapy of schizophrenic patients, cortical activity is gradually increased overcoming the protective inhibition. Disturbances in the bioelectric mozaic are found in divergent areas of the brain in different forms of schizophrenia and the depressions. Clinical changes brought about by psychotropic drugs are accompanied by rectification of these disturbances toward normal bioelectric activity.

The work of present-day scientists on interoceptive conditioning is bringing the arena of the "unconscious" to more direct experimental control and examination within a behavioral framework (Razran, 1961). Bykov (1957) demonstrated that the secretory reactions of the kidney, thyroid, and other organs, as well as blood and metabolic reactions, may become conditioned to a variety of stimuli. Later investigators observed that feelings of anxiety, or any of its visceromotor concomitants, may become conditioned stimuli for such disorders as constipation; constipation in turn being capable of acting as a conditioned stimulus to initiate anxiety, hypertension and other functional disturbances. Verbal stimuli, over a wide semantic spectrum, have also been joined to an array of somatic and visceral responses, both initiating and modifying them. This has opened the door to an understanding of how insight may operate in altering physiological patterns. For example, through complex conditioning techniques it has been possible to demonstrate how voluntary control may be exercised over involuntary processes. A subject who is brought to an understanding of the procedures and mechanisms involved may be trained to control his pupillary contractions and dilations by giving himself the appropriate signals. Gantt (1965) contends that any body function that has a representation in the central nervous system may be subjected to conditioning. He has also shown in dogs that the mere presence of a person may be linked to a resolution of neurotic cardiac and hypertensive symptoms. This would seem to have implications for the helping and psychotherapeutic processes. Emotional difficulties are regarded by neurophysiologists as conditioned autonomic reactions to stress which generalize to a wide variety of stimuli, even to words and to people. Potentially they may be extinguished through verbal and interpersonal conditionings.

Both Gantt ((1965) and Liddell (1965) have shown through animal experiments that while the central part of the conditioning process extinguishes relatively rapidly, the autonomic modalities persist. This is an important concept in explaining why some anxiety responses remain even when the person has clarified for himself the basis for the original conditioning distortions. At the same time hope is being awakened by experiments in interoceptive conditioning, such as those reported above, which demonstrate that it is possible to regulate certain autonomic constituents through verbal conditioning.

In addition to classical Pavlovian conditioning, the technique of free operant (instrumental) conditioning, originally developed by Skinner (1938, 1953, 1962) and modified by Lindsley (1956), has been employed as a means of behavioral measurement and control. A hungry rat put in a Skinner Box will develop a pattern of pressing a bar if as a result of such action a pellet of food is delivered to him at least part of the time. This pellet provides reinforcement for the current behavior which will continue as long as reinforcement is present. Human beings who have been placed in cubicles resembling the Skinner Box have exhibited precisely the same reactions lending feasibility to the method in studying human behavior (Lindsley, 1956, 1960).

Self-stimulation experiments on animals have been performed to locate the nerve sites of positive and negative reinforcements.

Positive reinforcers (pleasure centers) have been found in a cylindrical path of tissue on each side of the brain, from the forebrain through the lateral hypothalamus into the ventral midbrain. Electrodes placed in the lateral hypothalamus will cause rats to stimulate themselves at rates as high as 8,000 per hour until they drop from exhaustion. Negative reinforcers (pain centers) are situated in the midbrain, reticular formation, ventromedial portions of the thalamus, and some parts of the hippocampus, amygdala and ventral surface of the hypothalamus. Animals avoid the levers that stimulate these areas.

Since the centers for fear, attack, pleasure, pain, hunger and sex are situated in contiguous areas of the hypothalamus and limbic system, the question arises as to whether an intensive response in one focal zone may not irradiate into adjacent areas activating other foci. Can a strong stimulus promoting intense rage flood the hypothalamus with excitations that incite the nuclei associated with sexual feeling? If the answer to this question is positive, it may provide a neurophysiological explanation for the so-called "fusion of instincts" clarifying how impulses of aggression, sexuality, hunger, pleasure and pain become intermixed and eventually conditioned to each other. Under such circumstances excitations associated with one drive may flood over into neurons which control another drive when, because of intense need, the thresholds for discharge in the latter are low. It is possible also that at certain metabolic phases biochemical conditions in the hypothalamus encourage irradiation. This is not to eliminate higher level symbolic conditionings which can produce similar fusions of response which are explicable on a psychological basis. Psychoanalytic exploration and working through would in the latter instance perhaps prove of value, but in the former, yield meager results.

Response patterns become highly elaborated and even distorted through social conditioning. The releasing agencies, too, generalize to a variety of conditioned stimuli that may have little relationship to the original "releasers." In this way, sexual, aggressive, fearful, pleasureable and painful responses may be set off by a host of stimuli. Indeed stimuli customarily associated with basic reactions may not suffice to bring them about. On the other hand seemingly unrelated conditioned stimuli may produce them. Thus a child forced to eat by anxious parents may develop habits of nausea and vomiting at the sight of food. Material rewards and bribes may, however, motivate him to eat and to retain food, and these reinforcers may become the only stimuli to which he will respond. Similarly fear, aggression and sexual desire may become conditioned to adventitious perceptual and conceptual stimuli. Moreover a variety of conditioned physiological, symbolic and motor responses may develop that bear little outward resemblance to, but are substitutive for, inner impulses such as sexuality and aggression.

Experimental animal studies. A great deal may be learned about the functioning of the human brain by studies of the brains and behavior of lower animals. While one cannot safely transfer all data from any one species to another, experimental work with lower animals supplies us with a rich resource of hypotheses that lend themselves to experimental and clinical testing and verification.

Liddel's (1965) experiments in the conditioning of hundreds of sheep and goats, Gantt's (1960) work with dogs, and Masserman's (1943) with cats have shown the objective manifestations of experimental neuroses to be basically similar in animals and humans. Behavior becomes disorganized; limitations are imposed on ways of meeting the total life situation in its historical continuity; and disturbed physiological, growth and behavioral patterns persist for years and decades, not extinguishing with rest. Two types of response may be induced through Pavlovian conditioning: the first, brought about by regularly spaced signals, of over-reaction of the parasympathetic nervous system, fostering behavioral rigidity; and the second, promoted by signals spaced at various intervals, of exaggerated activity of the sympathetic nervous system, with behavioral volatility. Another observation is that the presence of the experimenter markedly influences the reaction of the animal. Even more interesting is the finding in young animals with experimental neuroses that a neurotic animal that runs alone will die within a few months or a year, while a neurotic sibling who runs with its mother will not. The mutual interactions of young animals and their mothers have led to observations on constructive operant conditioning which apparently serves to protect the animals from the traumatic effects of Pavlovian conditioning experiments, even to the point of preventing the development of experimental neuroses.

Masserman (1943, 1945, 1959) has outlined four biodynamic principles governing animal behavior. These consist of the following: (1) All behavior is motivated by physiological needs (motivation). (2) Organisms react not to an absolute reality, but to an interpretation of the milieu in terms of their own experiences (adaptation). (3) The blocking of goal-directed activities results in substitutive modes of reaching the same objective (displacement). (4) Two motivations appearing simultaneously in serious opposition with each other will clash, initiating internal tension (anxiety), resulting in ambivalent somatic and motor behavior, in substitutive and maladaptive tendencies (neuroses?) and/or regressive, disorganized and bizarrely symbolic activities (psychoses?).

By producing experimental neuroses in animals it may be possible to investigate various ways of ameliorating and curing them. This should supply important leads in approaching human neurosis. Among the techniques employed by Masserman (1965) are the following which were successful in different degrees and combinations:

1. *Change of milieu.* Prolonged rest in a favorable environment removed from the conflictual situation results in a reduction of fear and neurotic symptoms in the animal. Return to the laboratory is, however, followed by the reappearance of deviant patterns. Even though human beings tend to generalize neurotic reactions, removing them from the source of their conflict will tend to have a temporary beneficial effect, which may become more permanent if the respite is accompanied by psychotherapy or other corrective emotional experience. Coming back into the conflict situation, or another situation that symbolically represents it, will usually revive the emotional disorder.

2. *Satiation of a conflictual need.* A neurotic animal to whom food has become phobic may be forced to partake of food if it is made particularly attractive and openly available, or if the animal is forcibly tube fed so that its hunger becomes mitigated. In some cases this is accompanied by a corresponding decrease in other

neurotic manifestations. Unfortunately, this maneuver is not always successful, some animals continuing to react with avoidance responses or with an actual increase in the phobia. Forcing a person paralyzed by anxiety into a course of action calculated to satisfy one of his conflictual needs may in some instances result in a breakthrough of his paralysis. On the other hand, it may tend to activate his anxiety.

3. *Forced solution.* Bringing a hungry neurotic cat closer and closer to the apparatus forcefully until its head touches the pellets sometimes results in a sudden lunging at the food. Lesser and lesser degrees of "persuasion" are necessary until the food inhibition disappears completely. This technique may have some counterparts in the human management of a neurosis where, for instance, a child with a school phobia is exhorted and even forced to attend school in company with a parent who gradually removes herself from the scene.

4. *Example of normal behavior.* A phobic animal paired with a well-trained normal animal who works the switches with facility, may, after several days of observation, cautiously approach the food box and finally emulate the normal animal. In the same way neurotic children brought up in a milieu of "normal" youngsters may gradually, especially if their behavior is rewarded, approximate the deameanor of the other children.

5. *Reeducation by a trusted mentor.* If an experimenter is capable of developing a relationship with a neurotic animal (animals in fear are often regressively dependent) he may be able, step by step, to retrain the animal by exposing him slowly to increasingly larger increments of the anxiety stimulus. Thus he may get the animal to take food from his hand, next to accept food from the apparatus, then to open the box while the experimenter stands nearby, finally to work the switch and feed himself without further "support" from the therapist. This process of deconditioning is probably an aspect of all learning; it certainly comes into play in dealing with human neuroses. A person with anxiety is regressively dependent upon the therapist whom he tends to trust in his search for surcease from anxiety. The therapist utilizes the relationship either to bring the patient to an awareness of his conflict in the hope that the patient will begin to rehabilitate himself; or he may guide the patient toward correc-

tive experiences which possess increasingly greater potentials for overcoming anxiety. Sometimes he may actually desensitize the patient, as in the behavior therapies, by active conditioning techniques.

6. *Physio-pharmacologic methods.* Drugs, electroshock and lobotomy have been employed experimentally in neurotic animals. Some of the drugs act by dulling perception and preventing the development of elaborate associations, while disorganizing complex behavior patterns that are already formed. Thus animals under the influence of alcohol, bromides, barbiturates and some of the opiates will be less susceptible to techniques designed to induce experimental neuroses. Animals made neurotic by adaptational conflicts apparently dissociate their recently acquired fears under the influence of drugs, temporarily "forgetting" their inhibitions, phobias, defensive compulsions and regressions, slowly working simple switches as they had done prior to the induction of the neurosis. Some animals that experience relief from tensions while intoxicated develop a liking for alcohol, preferring it to food. The various tranquilizer drugs are less predictably effective than barbiturates and alchohol. Analogies with human neuroses are too obvious to need delineation. Sedatives, hypnotics and intoxicants are universally employed by mankind as a way of dulling perceptions, permitting the conquest of anxiety laden situations and an escape from inner problems. The implications for psychotherapy relate to the possibility of helping a patient master sufficient amounts of his turmoil through the intake of drugs to face his difficulties and to overcome the anxiety associated with them. Electroshock administered to a neurotic animal acts very much like an intoxicant drug, disintegrating complex and recently acquired disorganizing patterns of behavior. However, animals that have been subjected to electroshock show a permanently impaired capacity for complex learning, though this cannot be correlated with pathological changes in the brain detectable by any of the methods available today. In uncontrollable human anxiety, electroshock similarly may, at least temporarily, enable the individual to function comparatively free from stress, mastering situations from which he has removed himself because of anxiety. Basic patterns of behavior may also be altered by certain cerebral operations. This results in a transient disorganization of

perceptive and reactive patterns and a change in the individual's responsive capacities. Thus lesions in the ventro-medial thalami or amygdalae, and to some extent in the cingulate gyri, may disorganize experimentally produced neurotic patterns to the behavioral benefit of the animal. Interestingly, the effect of identical lesions in different animals will be contingent upon the unique experiences of each animal. For instance, lesions produced in the dorso-medial nucleus of the thalamus in normal cats impair to some extent their acquired skills and learning ability, but make them relatively passive and friendly. On the other hand, lesions of an identical nature in experimentally neurotic cats, while having the same effect on learning behavior, release patterns of hostility and overt aggression. Bilateral amygdaloid lesions in kittens or young monkeys produce much greater degrees of disorganization and diffusely erotic aggressive and unrealistic behavior than in adult animals. Certain patterns may be altered by specific cerebral lesions. Sectioning of the head of the caudate, or under Area 13 in the posterior orbital gyrus, releases spontaneity and responsive activity, overcoming otiosity, but sometimes going on to the extreme of vicious rage. On the other hand, lesions in the ventral thalamic-cingulate-hippocampal-amygdaloid circuits of the visceral brain may eliminate even dangerously aggressive behavior. Again the effect of identical lesions in different animals will vary with the experiences of the animals. The implications for human beings are to the effect that all people are constituted differently at birth, and because of their unique experiences will react variantly to cerebral lesions (and perhaps also to drugs). They will need treatment that is especially designed to their constitution and personality structure.

V

Stress and Adaptation

THERE IS NO BETTER EXAMPLE OF HOW CONDITIONED, COORDI-
nated activities of neurophysiological, biochemical and psychological systems influence adaptation than the organism's reaction
to stress. Stressful stimuli both from within and outside are constantly impinging on the individual, upsetting his equilibrium
and precipitating physiological and behavioral reactions whose
purpose it is to restore homeostasis.

Crucial for the harmonizing of the different systems toward
restoration of homeostasis, and the eventual mediation of the
stressful circumstance, is the great computer and data processing
apparatus of the body, the neocortex. Through multisynaptic
connections stressful stimuli influence the reticular formation
and hypothalamus. Impulses are then transmitted to other structures including the neocortex which processes and synthesizes the
information, codifying perceptions in terms of their symbolic
significance, and organizing coping mechanisms as a basis for
adaptive action. Physiological responses, concerned with regulation of the internal environment through the autonomic nervous
system, and behavioral activities, related to the external environment through the somatomotor nerves, are brought into play as
parcels of the adjustment repertoire of the organism. So long as
the individual is capable of coping with his current life situation;
so long as he can gratify his most important needs and dispose of
others he is unable to satisfy; so long as he can sustain a sense of
security and feelings of self-esteem; and so long as he is able to
mediate troubles that vex him, he will be able to keep himself in
a reasonable state of adaptive balance.

Where, however, this is not possible, as, for instance, when his
environment imposes on him burdens in excess of his reserves;
when he is unable to gratify basic needs; when his security is

48

threatened and his self-esteem shattered; and when conflict, defying resolution, torments him beyond endurance, the person will experience a threat to his adaptation. This threat, registered in altered homeostasis, is generally expressed as a state of tension. Tension affects the viscera, the skeletal musculature and the psychic apparatus. The individual responds by attempting to alleviate the impact of tension as well as by neutralizing its source if this is known to him. Such strivings, if successful, restore homeostasis.

Frequently, however, strivings directed at tension fail to reestablish homeostasis. This is usually the case where the sources of tension are unknown to the person or where reparative efforts to deaden it prove ineffectual. Under these circumstances the individual's sense of mastery may be jeopardized, giving rise to feelings of helplessness and catastrophic expectations of injury or destruction. Resultant is the experience of anxiety.

Anxiety is a physiological and psychic upheaval which shocks the organism into a variety of reactions, for anxiety is perhaps the most intolerable of all stressful human experiences, escape from which constitutes one of life's prime motivations.

Darwin's description of the fear response (Crile, 1915) is a colorful delineation of what happens also in the state of anxiety: "The heart beats quickly and violently, so that it palpitates or knocks against the ribs. . . . That the skin is much affected under the sense of great fear we see in the marvelous and inexplicable manner in which perspiration immediately exudes from it. The exudation is all the more remarkable as the surface is then cold, and hence the term, 'a cold sweat' whereas the sudorific glands are properly excited into action when the surface is heated. The hairs also on the skin stand erect, and the superficial muscles shiver. In connection with the disturbed action of the heart, the breathing is hurried. The salivary glands act imperfectly; the mouth becomes dry, and is often opened and shut. I have also noticed that under slight fear there is a strong tendency to yawn. One of the best-marked symptoms is the trembling of all the muscles of the body; and this is often first seen in the lips. From this cause, and from the dryness of the mouth, the voice becomes husky and indistinct, or may altogether fail. . . . As fear increases into agony of terror, we behold, as under all violent emotions, diversified results. The heart beats wildly, or may fail to act and faintness ensues; there is a death-like pallor; the breathing is labored; the wings of the nostrils are widely dilated; 'there is a gasping and convulsive motion of the lips, a tremor on the hollow cheek, a gulping and catching of the throat'; the uncovered and protruding eyeballs are fixed on the object of terror; or they may roll restlessly from side to side. . . . The pupils are said to be enormously dilated. All the muscles of the body may become rigid, or may be thrown into convulsive movements. The hands are alternately clenched and opened, often with a twitching movement. The arms may be protruded, as if to avert some dreadful danger, or may be thrown wildly over the head. . . . In other cases there is a sudden and uncontrollable tendency to headlong flight; and so strong is this that the boldest soldiers may be seized with a sudden panic. As fear rises to an extreme pitch, the dreadful scream of terror is heard. Great beads of sweat stand on the skin. All the muscles of the body are relaxed. Utter prostration soon follows, and the mental powers fail. The intestines are affected. The sphincter muscles cease to act and no longer retain the contents of the body. . . ."

The exact mechanism of the organism's reactions in initiating and responding to anxiety is not entirely known, although Selye (1950, 1956, 1961) has offered an interesting hypothesis which may furnish some clues. Selye contends that any kind of stress registers itself on the organism initially by a temporary "shock phase" ("alarm reaction") characterized by hypotension and lowered muscular tone. This leads to "counter-shock" and "resistance" responses induced by hypothalamic and autonomic stimulation. One effect of this, we can assume, is an excitation of the sympathetic–adrenal medullary system with an outpouring of norepinephrine and epinephrine. This causes sweating, increased pulse rate, increased blood pressure and increased muscle tonus. Also catalyzed are feelings of apprehension, tension and anxiety which then become additional, and ultimately principal stress sources. Hypothalamic-hypophysial-adrenal-cortical stimulation produces a release of corticosteroids and mineral corticoids (cortisone, hydrocortisone, adrenosterone, desoxycorticosterone, etc.) which circulate throughout the body and profoundly affect the glucose and mineral metabolism. The physiological purpose of this massive stimulation is to prepare the individual for the damage foisted on him by the stress stimulus. The reaction is a nonspecific one, and can be provoked by any source which upsets the homeostatic equilibrium of the body. Thus, being injured in an automobile accident, becoming ill with a febrile disease, or phantasies of injury at the hands of punitive authority will stimulate identical physiological stress responses.

Stress is accompanied by alterations in adrenocortical and thyroid function (Board et al. 1956), by the increased excretion of such substances as epinephrine, norepinephrine, electrolytes and creatinine, and by shifts in the enzyme systems. The adaptive role of such chemicals in preparing the individual for emergencies, and for the resolution of the stress situation, is undisputed. What is of theoretical concern, however, is the integrity of organization of the neural systems, particularly the reticular activating, limbic and hypothalamic systems, and the endocrine glands and autonomic nervous system that sponsor these adaptive biochemical reactions. Important too is the ability of the individual to dispose of the catabolic end products of stress which, of course, involves the integrity of his enzyme systems. Defects in these systems will register themselves in the organism's reaction to stress and will determine how adequately stress is resolved. The higher brain centers are directly involved in the stress reaction either through the perceptual apparatus, as in the case of external stress, or through subcortical–cortical pathways.

The "orienting reflex" plays an important role in stress in coordinating cortical, subcortical, visceral and somatic mechanisms in the interests of adaptation. Any new or discordant stimulus will bring this reflex into play. According to Sokolov (1960) a cell assembly exists in the cortex which preserves information about the modality, duration, intensity and presentation order of previous stimuli, deviations from which result in an activation of the brain stem reticular system, evoking the orienting reflex. This reaction is characterized by a state of alertness and attention, by coordinated movements of the body, head and eyes which augment the discriminative capacities of the cortical analyzers, leading to a gathering and synthesizing of information regarding the properties of the evocative stimulus toward its adaptive disposal or control. Physical changes of a visceral and somatic nature, brought about by excitation of the reticular, limbic and hypothalamic systems, include vasodilation of the cerebral vessels, vasoconstriction of the finger vessels, and alterations in respiration and heart rate to prepare the individual for any required action. Accompanying these changes are a galvanic skin response and a generalized electroencephalographic arousal reaction or blocking of the alpha rhythm by low voltage fast discharges. On the other hand, when stimuli are familiar and not stressful, the cortical brain assembly will not trigger the orienting reflex. Instead it will relay inhibitory impulses to the reticular formation to discourage any reactions.

Stimulation of the cortex is of survival value in higher animals, for the complexity of the environment necessitates elaborate adjustments which can be organized only by the participation of the higher psychic centers. Perceptual or conceptual awareness of the stress circumstance mobilizes psychic mechanisms of defense in line with past successful adaptations. The choice of defense reflects both the common defense mechanisms adopted by the group to which the individual belongs, and the unique familial and social patterns to which he has personally been exposed.

The consequence of these physiological and psychic maneuvers may be a resolution of stress and a restoration of homeostasis. This is an adaptive response. Where homeostasis does not occur, the continuing stress will keep provoking the same chain reaction with excitation of a constant physiological and psychic uproar. Stress symbols become affiliated with past symbolizations of turmoil and act as conditioned stimuli setting off new bouts of anxiety. Where no adaptive responses eventuate to reduce anxiety, it may set off stereotyped behavior patterns (regressive infantile, neurotic, and psychotic) that serve no useful purpose, indeed that prevent an appropriate adjustment immersing the individual in even greater difficulties than before.

Visceral symptoms are the product of a massive automatic situation brought about by anxiety. Changes occur in the smooth musculature and in glands throughout the body. Furthermore, a lowered threshold to sensory stimuli creates a generalized increase of reflex activity. Spasm of the cardiac and pyloric portions of the stomach, hyperchlorhydria, intestinal spasms, constipation or diarrhea are common phenomena. Changes in the tonus of vessels affect the blood distribution through the body. Cardiac responses include palpitations, tachycardia and extrasystoles. Spasm of the respiratory apparatus commonly develops. There may occur an alteration of secretions of the various organs, urinary frequency or retention, dysmenorrhea and other menstrual disorders. The general irritability and oversensitivity to stimuli are registered as paresthesias, hyperesthesias and defects of the higher sensory organs involving such functions as vision and hearing. There is an increased tonus of the striated musculature. This facilitates motor reactions, but, in prolonged states of stimulation, muscle spasms and tics interfere with proper functioning. Electrical measurement of skeletal muscles and peripheral nerves may show action potentials as very high, even in a resting state. Excitations penetrating the higher brain centers produce constellations of ideas, memories and fantasies associated with the state of unrest. A wide variety of symbolic material may be mobilized in this representation, depending upon individual experiences and upon the degree of repression that exists in relation to the specific needs or problems that produce stress.

Overstimulation resulting from *continued* stress is bound to register its effect on the bodily integrity ("exhaustion reaction"). Bombardment of the viscera with stimuli will tend after a while organically to disturb the functions of the various organs and systems. To such ensuing disturbances Selye has given the name "diseases of adaptation."

Where the sources of anxiety are known to the person, he will best be in a position to deal with them constructively through adaptive mechanisms of defense. Where the sources are unknown, as in unconscious conflict, the higher psychic apparatus is virtually obliterated as an adaptive tool. The person will then be handicapped in coping with anxiety, which, acting as a constant stress stimulus, will sabotage his adjustment on all levels of integration. Chart III, "Adaptation Syndrome," summaries the chief elements of the stress reaction.

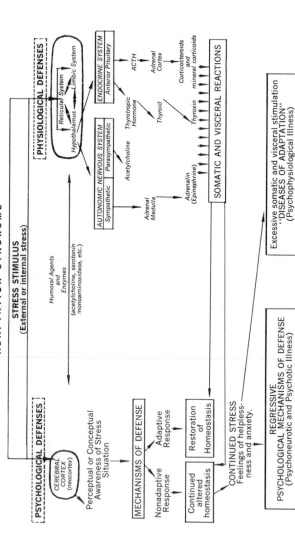

CHART III

ADAPTATION SYNDROME

Stress, irrespective of source, initiates a chain reaction in the individual aimed at restoring homeostasis. The stress stimulus acts upon both subcortical and cortical brain centers mobilizing physiological and psychological defenses. In coordination with the reticular and limbic systems, the hypothalamus becomes activated, some of its centers fostering excitation of the autonomic nervous system. Stimulation of the sympathetic division and the adrenal medulla causes an outpouring of epinephrine (adrenalin). The hypothalamus also provokes the anterior pituitary gland to secrete thyrotropic and adrenocorticotropic hormone (ACTH) which, in concert with epinephrine, influences the adrenal cortex to liberate corticosteroids that circulate throughout the body. Released endocrine substances, chemical products, like serotonin, acetylcholine, norepinephrine and epineph-

rine, and enzymes, such as mono-amine oxidase, induce an intensive physiological stimulation preparing the individual for whatever emergencies may lie ahead in dealing with the existing stress. Perceptual or conceptual awareness, through the higher cortical centers of the stress circumstance mobilizes psychic mechanisms of defense in line with past successful adaptations. The consequence of these physiological and psychic responses may be a resolution of stress and a restoration of homeostasis. Where this does not occur, altered homeostasis may linger with continued working of the adaptation syndrome. The persistence of stress may then foster neurotic and psychotic defenses, and the continuing physiological uproar may eventuate in damage to organs throughout the body in what Selye has described as "diseases of adaptation."

VI

Ontogenetic Maturation;
Developmental and Personality
Theories

THERE IS LITTLE QUESTION THAT THE CHILD ENTERS THE WORLD with a number of fixed motor patterns (Peiper, 1963). These include respiratory coordinations, neck and head maneuvers which aid the infant in the searching for the breast, lip movements which grasp the nipple and position it in the mouth, directional responses to tactile stimulation (rooting reflex), sucking and swallowing activities, movements which lead to rejection of the breast from the mouth, the startle (Moro) reflex, grasping motions of the fingers and thrashings of the legs and arms. The newborn baby also possesses innate patterns that communicate its needs to the mother and that enable him to respond to her stimulation. From the first day of life there is a capacity to orient to the environment, an ability to enter into a reciprocal relationship with the mother, and to incorporate the environment through whatever perceptual stimulations the developing sense organs are able to encompass. Locomotor movements (crawling, creeping, walking on fours, standing, ambulating on both feet) are apparently genetically determined. Neonates are capable of fishlike movements when placed in a prone position in water (McGraw, 1963), swimming forward while reflexly inhibiting breathing. Such movements, considered atavistic residuals, cease after a few months. Emotional responses (pleasure, fear, rage) possess hereditary substrates, as do neuromuscular responses to external stimuli and autonomic reactions to an unbalancing of the internal homeostasis.

Various attempts have been made with some success to chart the sequence of fixed motor patterns that progressively appear during the development of the child (Gesell and Amatruda, 1947). Cross cultural studies indicate that there is an orderly progression of locomotor and basic emotional patterns at set stages of growth irrespective of the society in which the individual is reared. Whether or not there is also uniform development of the personality structure in all cultures is subject to greater dispute, although some attempts have been made to delineate stages of personality growth (Piaget, 1955; Erikson, 1950, 1959). Interpretation of the data of development, however, varies. There are some authorities (ethologists, neurophysiologists, Freudian psychoanalysts) who uphold Haeckels "biogenetic law" to the effect that "ontogeny recapitulates phylogeny" and that the developing organism is an epitome of "form-modifications undergone by the successive ancestors of the species in the course of their historic evolution," and who support McDougall's (1908) contention that essentially the mainsprings of social behavior are rooted in instincts. There are others (sociologists, cultural anthropologists, neo-freudians) who insist that as the animal ascends the phyletic scale, innate patterns undergo extensive modification and even extinction, and are replaced by devious social conditionings. What is inherited are not specific behavioral configurations, but the capacity to respond to important cues in the environment which results in multiple learned patterns. These become autonomous drive sources, fulfillment of which is as vital to the individual as the unconditioned responses which characterize fixed motor constellations.

In the main, social scientists have decried the post-Darwinian emphasis on biology which presents man as essentially a creature of instinct relegated to fixed motor actions as mainsprings of behavior. Rather, they insist, social customs fashion human behavior in all of its dimensions. Contended is the fact that while instinct provides for behavior some motivational force, cultural influences contribute even more significantly to its manifold forms. This has given rise to a trend which promulgates a complete elimination of instinct as a significant factor in behavior and promotes society as the exclusive determining agency.

To this cultural emphasis biological scientists have responded with acknowledgement that acquired insightful patterns are present and important in man, but are merely superimposed upon the more basic innate stereotypes. However instinctual behavior is not made more plastic or susceptible to alteration through the impact of experience (Lorenz, 1937). Evidence for this viewpoint is presented in the observation that regressive and innate patterns come through with frightening intensity, often in their pristine form, when acquired mechanisms of defenses crumble as in severe mental illness.

New data from biology, genetics and ethology is available which points to the relative stability of certain behavioral patterns. These do not depend on learning or social acquisition, being determined by forces evolved during the general course of development for survival (Eiduson, 1958). While such instinctual promptings in man are materially tamed by environmental conditionings, the biological heritage does in all probability set the limit for the influences of experience. There is abundant evidence that man, like other animals, is endowed with innate impulses which cause him to respond differentially to environmental stimuli (Lorenz, 1952; Tinbergen, 1951, 1953, 1954, 1959, 1961; Harlow, 1960, 1962). The inducements to which man reacts are many and it is probable that responses to them are in terms of diffuse pleasure and pain rather than in specific fixed behavioral forms (McClelland, 1951, 1955, 1961, 1964).

Clinical studies on human infants indicate that innate characteristics determine individual differences at birth and lay down the basis for variations in sensitivity to stimuli, perception, motility, discrimination, anxiety and memory (Benjamin, 1961; Bergman and Escalone, 1949). These variables will undoubtedly influence the manner in which the infant is affected by this environment. For example, the intensity with which the infant experiences stress and the forcefulness of the protests by which he signals his needs are probably related to genetic factors. Where the child is unable to respond to hunger, pain, and discomfort appropriately, he may not give proper clues to his needs. Weak, indistinct and contradictory clues will not invoke the proper mothering responses, particularly from a mother who is emotionally disturbed and preoccupied with her own problems (Bruch, 1964). The failure of the mother to provide proper help will deprive the child of the essential feeling of trustingness, and of proper indentification and separation experiences that make it possible to differentiate the "me" from the "not-me." This is but one instance of how nature and nurture interact. Differential protective barriers against stimuli as well as homeostatic stress-response patterns exist at birth which appear to influence the development of personality, cognitive style, interpersonal relations, defense mechanisms and other psychologic functions (Roche Report, June 1, 1964). Important to consider also is the fact that a mother may respond differently to an irritable crying baby as compared with a placid and easily manageable one.

Innate constellations manifest themselves not only at birth, but also in chronological sequence following birth in line with set laws of maturation. Some patterns are related to the development of the central nervous system and to the progressive myelinization of nerve tracts. Others follow the ripening of certain organs, like the hormonal glands. Throughout life physical changes appear to sponsor special psychological activities.

A finding, suggested by animal studies, which has profound implications for psychotherapy is that the neural system becomes susceptible to the imprinting of certain stimuli for only limited periods during the life cycle (Hesse, 1959). Beyond this period the necessary imprinting does not take place even upon exposure to identical stimulation. Thus among monkeys it has been shown that separation of an infant from the mother during the first few weeks in life, and isolation from other monkeys, may produce damage from which the animal never recovers even though it is returned to the mother following the limited separation span. Disturbances such as withdrawal, fear and rage reactions will persist (Harlow, 1960, 1962). Among dogs the optimal imprinting period for the development of social bonds is from six to eight weeks of age. Contact with a handler during this period establishes a capacity for a relationship with humans and a ready breaking to the leash. If contact occurs later than eight weeks, the dogs tend to become fearful and resist training. Such phenomena are probably organically determined since specific biochemical changes in the brain have been reported during imprinting periods that are not present thereafter.

A reasonable assumption is that a human child may also never restitute himself from essential need deprivations or the absence of important growth experiences if such lacks are sustained at crucial phases in development. The sabotage to the evolving personality may be too drastic; no amount of therapy in later life can restore to the individual that which never existed. For example, if a child is severely neglected or abandoned during the first year, and therefore has never been supplied with a consistent mothering experience, it is probable that emotional apathy and a distrusting-ness of people may pursue him the remainder of his existence irrespective of how benevolent his environment may be afterward.

Cognitive processes. Freudian emphasis on primary process, energy exchange and unconscious motivation relegated cognition to a secondary role in personality structure and function. During the past few decades the holistic or molar concept of organization has tended to elevate man's symbolic processes to a more promi-nent position. Important toward this end has been the work of Tolman (1936) who described cognition as an intervening variable between the stimulus situation (the independent variable) and the resultant behavior (the dependent variable), as well as Gold-stein (1939) who emphasized the holistic dependence of all be-havior, arranged in hierarchial organization of function with cognition at the apex representing the environment abstractly through concepts. Of significance has been the work of Piaget (1952), Werner (1936), Angyall (1941), Leeper (1951) and many others including the Gestalt theorists, the field theorists, the phe-nomenologists, and the "ego analysts," who have contributed ideas of configuration and concepts of phenomenal fields to the organizational characteristics of cognitive representation, and have substantiated the vital position of cognition in adaptation. The emphasis on cognitive processes has been punctuated by informa-tion emerging from computer technology, communications theory and cybernetics which indicate that some emotional components of decision making may be imitated by the "intellectual" opera-tions of data processing instruments. The conclusion to be drawn from these studies is that social perception is subject to a definite cognitive structuring (Stern, 1938; Heider, 1944; Werner, 1948). Moreover the body image itself is a paradigm of cognitive repre-sentation outside of awareness (Scheerer, 1954).

It is largely to Piaget and his followers that we owe our under-standing of how cognitive processes develop during different phases of the child's growth (Maier, 1965; Piaget and Inhelder,

1958, 1964). Gradually we may observe a development from the original sensorimotor thinking ("exocept"), to early symbolization embodying images without distinguishing between inner and outer reality, to imageless thought processes ("endocept"), and, as language is acquired, to concrete, vague, paleological or prelogical thinking patterns ("predicate logic"), finally, to precise, abstract, integrated thought structures ("subject logic"). The interplay of symbolic imagery and language establishes meaning for the acquisition and fixation of further information. Operational behavior is modulated by the use of language; images become progressively mobile and language more structured. The evolution of adult thinking patterns is obviously vital to the adjustment of the individual, influencing behavior on all levels. The study of such patterns is best approached in a developmental perspective. The recent work of Piaget and Inhelder on pre-psychotic, dyspraxic, dyslexic and dysphasic children and adolescents, on mental retardates, and on senile dementia demonstrates this by showing that cognitive operations disintegrate in an inverse order to their developmental evolution.

Clinical investigations indicate that the faulty evolvement of cognitive processes in childhood has serious effects on the general formation of personality. For example, perceptual distortions in brain injured children have been shown to foster conceptual lability, with hyperactivity and distractibility (Gallagher, 1962; Bender, L., 1956; Strauss and Lehtinen, 1947, 1955). Where an impairment in visual and auditory channels exists, the incoming data will not be decoded or encoded accurately. Defects will be registered in attention, motivation, cortical integration, orientation, language formation, expressive speech, motor performance and general adaptability.

Impairments are also present in children who are not brain injured, but whose upbringing is experientially impoverished during the first year of life. Distortions are reflected in defects in perception, logic, problem solving, motivation, communication and social behavior. Such cognitive difficulties result in faulty generalizations and chaotic organization of systems within the individual that act as potent sources of conflict. There is a failure to identify and to act appropriately toward traumatic stimuli. Cognitive maneuvers thus structure the individual's world and are constantly interacting with emotional processes. A holistic view-point that integrates the various operative dimensions of the human being presents itself as the best approach to personality development, organization and disorganization.

Summary. A synthesis of studies in the biological and social fields leads to the following propositions relevant to personality theory:

(1) The task of human growth is to transform an amorphous creature, the infant, into a civilized adult capable of living adaptively in a complex social framework. Toward this end the child cultivates restraints on his biological impulses, develops symbol manipulating communicative facilities, acquires skills in interpersonal relationships, evolves values that are consonant with the society in which he lives and perfects techniques that allow him to fulfill himself creatively within the bounds of his potentials.

(2) Growth is governed by a number of developmental laws; for instance, laws of maturation which give rise to inherited units of response during critical periods of development common to the entire human species, laws peculiar to the cultural and subcultural group of which the individual is a part, and finally, laws unique to himself, parcels of his personal experience that will make his development unlike that of any other individual.

(3) While growth is broadly similar in all human infants and children, there is great difference in individual styles and the rate of growth.

(4) Development may conveniently be divided into a number of stages of growth corresponding roughly with certain age levels (see Chart IV). While there is some variation in timing and rate, the average individual appears to follow these stages with surprising sequential regularity.

(5) The various stages are characterized by specific needs that must be propitiated, common stresses that must be resolved and special skills that must be developed. A healthy personality structure develops on the basis of the adequacy with which these needs are supplied, stresses mastered and skills learned at progressive age levels.

(6) Difficulties may arise at each stage of growth that engender a partial or complete failure in the satisfaction of needs, the solu-

CHART IV

PERSONALITY DEVELOPMENT
(see chart for corresponding numbers)

(1) Hereditary and constitutional elements are the building blocks of personality. Along with intrauterine influences they determine sensitivity and activity patterns and thus regulate the character of later conditionings. Under the promptings of maturation, needs emerge and skills evolve with surprising regularity. Environmental factors nevertheless may modify these prenatal forces and fashion the lines along which the personality structure is organized.

(2) Personality evolves out of the conditionings and experiences of the individual in his relationships with the world. Basic needs must be gratified and appropriate coping mechanisms evolved, the consummation of which, at any age level, if inadequate will retard and if satisfactory will expedite successive stages of growth. The social milieu, reflected in the disciplines and values sponsored by the family, designs the specific outlets for and modes of expression of the emerging needs.

(3) Personality maturation is contingent on execution of vital tasks which must be successfully fulfilled at the different age levels.

(4) What inhibits or distorts growth are depriving experiences which block the proper satisfaction of needs. An unwholesome milieu tends to foster destructive patterns that crush security, undermine self-esteem and interfere with the development of essential skills and values that are consonant with the requirements of adaptation.

(5) At any age level collapse in adaptation may be sponsored when basic needs are vitiated, and security and self-esteem are shattered with no hope of immediate reparation. If the reservoir of defenses is sufficiently flexible, considerable conflict may be endured. On the other hand, where the personality underpinnings are unstable, even minimal conflict may tax coping capacities. A combination of symptoms issues from failure to mediate conflicts, including, in the main, the various manifestations of anxiety, defenses against anxiety, as well as technics of counteracting or solving the conflictual situation itself. While the elaborated symptoms are unique for every individual, being influenced by the specific experiences of the person, and by the singular mechanisms of defense he has found successful in past dealings with stress, definite groupings of symptoms appear with sufficient frequency to constitute familiar syndromes. Symptomatic evidences of a failing adjustment may persist from one age level to the next, accretions of succeeding difficulties being added to or substituting for problems existing at preceeding age levels.

(6) Residues of defective rearing contaminate adjustment by influencing disorganizing relationships with other individuals. Conflict is thus in constant generation. The specific deposits of defect display themselves in luxuriant forms, the cumulative product of pathological accruals from one age level to the next.

(7) Awareness of formative experiences and elaborated defenses may be dimmed by repression. Forgetting or repudiating them does not protect the individual against their forays into his conscious life in direct or derivative form. Early conflicts may be revived symbolically in dreams, through the use of psychotomimetic drugs, as a result of an overpowering emotional crisis, during an intense relationship with a personage who represents a parental or sibling figure, or by a transference neurosis inspired in the course of psychotherapeutic treatment.

VII

Learning Theory
and Learning Principles

THE HUMAN ORGANISM IS, AS WE HAVE SEEN, PROGRAMMED TO
respond in life with a series of patterns consistent for the species.
Some of these innate configurations are present at birth; others
appear later according to a maturation schedule. Instinctual
mechanisms become modified through varied kinds of learning
until a rich sequence of patterns emerge which both regulate the
individual's relationships with his environment and with his inner
psychic and physiologic structures. Sensory, motor and affective
elements are bound together into a complex organization through
opulent conditionings which will, more or less, endure during the
lifetime of the individual. Relearning nevertheless may occur
altering even some of those patterns that seem indelibly recorded.

Among the most effective relearning experiences is exposure
to an interpersonal process prosecuted by a skilled psychotherapist.
Indeed psychotherapy is predicated on the principle that behavior
may be modified through learning. In essence this means the re-
placement of outmoded habits and disabling patterns with more
useful and propitious ones. It is posited that the principles of
learning must certainly apply to psychotherapy as they do to any
process that proposes to bring about behavior change or to enrich
the repertoire of interactive patterns. A corollary consideration
is, of course, the clinical finding that not all behavior is modifiable, at least not with the techniques that are currently available.
It is a confounding fact that certain kinds of behavior seem fixed
and irreversible despite exposure to relearning. First experiences
during infancy probably have an intense and perhaps even permanent effect on the individual if we are to accept the lessons of
ethology in relation to imprinting. Moreover, unless learning has

67

occurred at certain developmental epochs, essential characteristics may not be acquired before or after this period no matter how equitable the learning climate may be. For example, an affect-hungry child, deprived of essential love and stimulation during the first year of life may never be able to acquire feelings of trust and capacities for lovingness even in the most harmonious interpersonal environment. Another interesting observation is that certain kinds of learning are best accomplished in the medium of special interpersonal situations. Thus, some aberrant behavioral tendencies do not yield to verbal psychotherapy; yet they may respond to other less formal and less expensive procedures. For instance, a formal psychotherapeutic experience for the chronic alchoholic is generally not so effective as his joining an Alcoholics Anonymous group. Phobic situations may rapidly be dissipated by behavior therapy even where years of formal psychoanalysis have proven futile. Delinquent acting-out may actually be encouraged by permissive, accepting psychotherapeutic relationships; while it may be controlled and even influenced for the better in more disciplined settings.

Accepting the idea that psychotherapy involves the unlearning of old, destructive habit patterns and the learning of new and productive ones, can known principles of learning explain this process?

Immediately we must recognize that the precise operations by which habits are acquired are not explicit. Neural connections are laid down and are strengthened by the repeated passage of impulses. Through association and conditioning there evolve organizations of increasing complexity. To explain the existent operations, learning theories have been proposed.

Learning theories embody a number of not too congruent theories which presume to explain how behavior is altered by experience. At the present stage of knowledge, learning theory is capable of accounting for only restricted aspects of human behavior. Some of the current confusion arises from the fact that practically all of our present learning theories have emerged out of work with species below the order of man. Pavlov himself warned of coming to unwarranted conclusions in transferring findings from one species over to another. The kind of intelligence characteristic of man seems to have been considered by some learning theorists as an interfering and unwelcome intervening variable.

In the main, two large groupings of learning theories exist. First, there are a number of reactive and peripheralistic theories, like those of Clark Hull and Neal Miller, which credit learning to the factor of stimulus and sensory mechanisms affected by stimulus, i.e., to a stimulus-response correlation. Such associational learning theories deal with the continuous orderly connections of sensations, central processes and motor events, while reinforcement of the connections is insured by drive reduction (positive rewards or pain elimination). Second, there are cognitive theories, like those of Edward Tolman, and the Gestalt theorists, which, ascribing learning to intermediary central brain processes, insist that what is learned are cognitive structures rather than responses, i.e., an alteration in ways of perceiving. Learning is considered a product of the reorganization of a field, structured and restructured according to different sets of cues. Problem solving is a manifestation of the insightful remodeling of the conceptual field.

Between and within those two broad theoretical premises of the "reinforcement" and "expectancy" schools there is much controversy as to how learning actually takes place: through contiguity and association? (Guthrie, 1935); through reward and reinforcement? (Hull, 1951); through the dynamic field, and the principle of "pragnanz"? (Lewin, 1951); through instrumental behavior? (Skinner, 1938); through drive induction and drive reduction? (Mowrer, 1948); through neuropsychological correlates? (Hebb, 1949); through dynamic motivation? (Pearson, 1954). A study of the various learning theories (see Hilgard, 1956) indicates that we are still far from the day when we can pinpoint the true processes by which experience leads to psychic or behavioral change.

In spite of the dispute over learning theories, a number of notable attempts have been made to view psychotherapy in the light of learning theory. Dollard and Miller (1950), for example, have formulated some interesting hypotheses in stressing the learning factors involved in both the development of behavior and in bringing about behavior change. While their drive reduction theory does not explain all types of learning, it helps to clarify some aspects of conflict, particularly those of approach-avoidance, and the role of fear in human interactions. Mowrer (1950), Rotter (1954) and Kelly (1955) have also made contributions that are worthy of study. The least we can derive from such attempts to employ learning theory as a model for psychotherapy is to recognize that there is a relationship between learning and the operations that go on in the treatment situation.

Principles of learning. A great deal of experimental data is available on how organisms learn. An understanding of the basic principles of learning is useful toward understanding ways in which psychotherapy serves to reorganize habits.

Learning is a complex process which involves a number of coordinated operations including conditioning and the apprehension of new meanings and relationships. Conditioning phenomena, which incidentally extend over the entire phyletic gamut, and, in man, from fetal to geriatric periods, are of two classes: "respondent" and "operant," each influencing somewhat different aspects of behavior. *Respondent* or *classical conditioning,* originally described by Pavlov, consists of the presentation in close temporal proximity of two stimuli: (1) a stimulus (unconditioned stimulus "US") which has a reflex or previously established connection with a response (unconditioned response "UR") and (2) an unrelated stimulus (conditioned stimulus "CS"). After repeated paired presentations, the unrelated (conditioned) stimulus acquires the ability to evoke the same response (conditioned response "CR"). In this way a large number of conditioned stimuli, including words, perceptions, etc., become affiliated with physiological responses (reflexes such as heart rate, blood pressure, sweating, pupil dilation, salivation, hair erection, etc.) and emotions (fear, hate, pleasure, disgust, etc.). *Operant* or *instrumental conditioning* (Skinner, 1953), also called "trial-and-error learning," consists of the selection through experiment of responses that bring a reward in a specific situation. Complex skills and habits, such as learning to talk, are acquired in this way (Harlow, 1954; Olds, 1955; Miller, 1958). Operant conditioning is motivated by behavior instigators (drives) in the form of tissue needs (such as hunger, thirst, sexual stimulation) and aversive stimuli (discomfort, pain, tension, anxiety). Out of the diffuse responses to such drives there will be those that bring rewards of satisfying the tissue need or removing the aversive stimulus. The successful response will then tend to be repeated whenever the motive (drive) recurs. The establishment of responses in the form of habits that will continue indefinitely depends on a fixed schedule of "reinforcement" through incidental rewards ("positive reinforcers" which will encourage certain behavioral operations) and critical disapprobations ("negative reinforcers" that will discourage selected actions). The absence of such reinforcing stimuli will lead to instability in responses and perhaps to their extinction.

Conditioned stimuli tend to become generalized, although the magnitude of responses diminishes with the degree of how perceptually different a stimulus is from an original conditioned stimulus. Responses conditioned to a word may be elicited by other words which possess the same meaning to the individual as the conditioned stimulus word (semantic conditioning). Stimulus generalization may be restrained by the process of "discrimination" in which an affiliated conditioned stimulus is extinguished by being presented *without* the reinforcing unconditional stimulus, while the conditional stimulus to be reinforced is paired *with* the unconditioned stimulus.

The extinction of any conditioned responses is best brought about by presentation of the conditioned stimulus without reinforcement. Spontaneous recovery may occur, but scheduled repetition of unreinforcement will eventually lead to complete extinction. There is evidence that some responses, once acquired, may never be extinguished even though they are not openly expressed. In the latter case it is probable that subliminal reinforcement is present, as may be manifest in some early memories which, laying apparently dormant in the unconscious, can periodically be aroused. The passage of time itself is therefore not an extinguishing factor unless unreinforcement is coexistent. While failure to reward a response hastens its extinction, it is doubtful that punishment has this effect. Indeed punishment leads to disturbing side reactions. The painful consequences of a response may force a temporary inhibition of functioning, but once defenses against these consequences are elaborated, or withdrawal from the punitive agency takes place, the response is apt to come back, the devitalization produced by failure of positive reinforcement in the interim soon being dissipated. Extinction of anxiety is helped by gradual exposure of the individual, to the limit of his tolerance, to steadily increased increments of anxiety. Acceptance of less fearsome situations is followed by mastery of more powerful ones.

Human problem solving is associated with both trial-and-error and insightful activity. The problem situation is analyzed in terms of goals and subgoals utilizing the memory of related past problem situations. The goal is solved then in a piecemeal way, overcoming subproblems step by step. This "means-end" analysis is supplemented by utilizing "rules of thumb" to reduce the size of the problem so that it can then be more easily approached through trial-and-error. Where there are few available rules of thumb, as in a novel problem situation, a trial-and-error search will be extensive, almost random. Where the situation is familiar, rules of thumb are available and solutions may be almost immediate with little search.

Application of learning principles to psychotherapy. A number of practical conclusions derive from studies on learning.

1. *Motivation: Motivational forces in the form of anticipating rewards and eliminating pain vitally influence the acquisition of new habits.* Learning accompanied by pleasurable responses, and by reactions that relieve suffering, will be reinforced. Learning accompanied and followed by pain and distress will tend to be forgotten.

Among the most powerful of motivants for relearning in psychotherapy is a certain degree of symptomatic suffering as well as recognition that one is living below his potential and hence not receiving due rewards.

During therapy, motivation is provided in the patient's need to eliminate anxiety and disabling symptoms, and to anticipate a more productive adjustment and greater interpersonal happiness. Such incentives are neutralized by the safety and secondary gain values of the neurosis which act as positive reinforcers for neurotic responses. In his operations, the therapist tries to undermine the secondary values of the patient's symptoms and defenses by emphasizing their destructive qualities. He also encourages all efforts on the part of the patient to acquire new patterns by pointing out the rewards that will accrue from changes in behavior. The initial relief from tension as a result of the placebo factor, the relationship dimension, emotional catharsis and the effect of suggestion serve as motivants to keep the patient in treatment until he can achieve more substantial gains. Approving utterances and gestures from the therapist act to direct the patient's associations and behavior along advantageous lines. The mastery of symptoms, and the development of new and useful responses act as further motivants reinforcing utilitarian behavior patterns.

2. *Reduction of anxiety: The emotion of fear and anxiety upon presentation of certain cues is one of the most inhibiting factors in constructive learning.* It is responsible for a host of avoidance responses as well as for other kinds of disorganizing defenses. The reduction of anxiety, is therefore, a goal in all learning.

The therapist deals with the defenses against anxiety in quest of exposing the emotion and exploring its source. In an atmosphere of permissiveness and acceptance he encourages verbalization, and he focuses the interview on anxiety laden areas the patient seeks to circumvent (resistance). As the patient delves into the pockets of his misery and learns he can tolerate some anxiety without disintegration, he identifies some of its roots. Misconceptions are clarified. Hostilities and guilt feelings are explored in an accepting atmosphere shorn of retaliatory punishment. Emotional catharsis lessens anxiety, and an understanding of its meaning helps to subdue its paralyzing quality, encouraging new and better defenses. In this way the patient is helped to tolerate progressively increasingly anxiety laden thoughts, ideas and acts. In the behavior therapies, insight into the sources of anxiety is not considered essential to the extinction process. Various techniques recondition the fear inspiring ideas and situations to positive affects.

3. *Extinction of disturbed patterns: If a conditioned stimulus is not reinforced, the magnitude of the conditioned response will progressively diminish and the response will ultimately disappear.* If the extinction process goes on for a short period only a rest period will usually lead to spontaneous recovery. Further presentations then of the conditioned stimulus without reinforcement will bring about a rapid extinction. This back and forth extinction and spontaneous revival are characteristic of operant habits.

So long as there is no intermittent reinforcement, extinction will ultimately prevail.

Aberrant social habits, coping mechanisms, symptoms and defensive maneuvers are the consequence of destructive conditionings and indiscriminate intermittent reinforcements which lead to a medley of disturbed stimulus and response generalizations. The extinction of these conditionings and generalizations constitutes an essential first element in overcoming a neurosis. During therapy the patient gains a clearer awareness of maladaptive responses and their symbolic extensions (symptoms, character traits, etc.) as well as the reinforcements in his environment and in himself that keep them alive. Interpretation by the therapist of the meaning of his responses and their effects on him, and approbatory reactions and mild disapprobatory comments, such as challenging questions or interpretations whenever destructive behavior is reported, tends to negate their reinforcement. Constancy in blocking reinforcement is supported by a continuous schedule of treatment appointments. Resistance to the extinction process must consistently be handled by the therapist so that the patient does not relapse into his old habits. Alertness never to abandon a regular schedule of unreinforcement is needed, since intermittent reinforcement will tend to negate effects. As the patient identifies with the therapist and incorporates his ideas and standards, his value systems will tend to undergo alteration. On the one hand, his conscience (superego) will tolerate better the expression of drives that have been repudiated because of guilt and anxiety (drive intensification). On the other, it will encourage inhibition of disorganizing responses that are compulsive and repetitive (drive reduction). The individual himself will therefore be able to replace the therapist as the reinforcing and unreinforcing agency and he will gradually extinguish his own neurotic responses provided he does not intermittently reward them. Proper psychotherapy equips the patient to alert himself to the contingency of relapse into his old habits, to an awareness of the deviousness of neurotic strivings and the symbolic disguises they assume in new contexts, and to avoid reinforcing them should such tendencies reappear.

4. *Response selection: Learning is enhanced by the proper selection of responses. Behavior sequences associated with a negative*

affect tend to be inhibited and extinguished (Hull, 1943; Spence, 1956). Learning here occurs through continuity with response termination (drive reduction), being encouraged by responses that bring about the termination of tension, pain, fear or anxiety. Circumstances that block or remove such upsetting feelings or deleterious reactions to them are apt to be repeated and learned. *At the same time behavior sequences associated with a positive affect tend to recur and become habitual.* Learning here takes place in continuity with response arousal (drive intensification). A "shaping" toward a desired goal is effectuated by reinforcements given to responses that are at first only remotely related to a selected objective and then more and more pointedly affiliated.

The therapist helps the patient to select proper responses in his thinking and actions that will lead both to an ablation of anxiety and to the enhancement of adaptive behavior. He does this by providing the patient with cues that enable the latter to organize new modes of perceiving reality and of relating to his environment. Reinforcements in the form of approval and dis-approval, explicit and implicit, verbal and nonverbal, are pro-vided for responses that are constructive (thoughts, judgements, acts, etc.). At first, reinforcements are given to reactions that *approximate* desirable behavior, since a complete adjustment may not yet be in the patient's repertory. The variability of the patient's conduct is thus reduced, and, as reinforcement is given only to aspects that approach closer and closer to healthy actions, a shaping of behavior toward "normality" eventuates. The thera-pist continues to alert himself to responses that result in adapta-tion. He helps the patient to see the value in perpetuating those. Coordinately he undermines any masochistic need to continue tension arousing behavior by exploring its origins and purpose. He interprets resistances to the awareness and experiencing of pleasurable feelings or productive actions. Extinction of symp-toms and a conditioning of positive thoughts and acts to pleasure feelings is directly attempted in the behavior therapies without the formality of self-awareness.

5. *Reinforcement: Responses that are followed in close tem-poral sequence with a reinforcing stimulus will increase in strength.* In therapy, certain responses, such as positive ideas and constructive actions, are encouraged through reinforcing rewards,

such as expressions of acceptance or approval (verbal or non-verbal) when the patient makes certain ideational associations or acts in assertive ways. Negative reinforcers in the form of very *mild* reprimand or expressions of disapproval from the therapist will tend to discourage destructive impulses and behavior, *provided there is a good relationship with the therapist.* Reinforcements are made as close to sanctioned responses as possible. This contiguity enhances operant learning. Reinforcement schedules are regularly maintained by uniformly spaced sessions during which the therapist exhorts the patient to continue responses that are in the interests of his getting well. As the values of the patient change, he becomes capable of arbitrating the reinforcement of his own constructive responses without the help of the therapist.

6. *Stimulus and response generalization: Once a stimulus produces a goal directed response, similar stimuli will tend to elicit the same response (primary stimulus generalization).* To a lesser extent, stimuli that are not perceptually alike, but which have independently produced similar responses will tend to be generalized (mediate stimulus generalization). Once a response is learned in relation to a given stimulus, the same type of stimulus, or a stimulus with the same kind of meaning will elicit similar responses, (response generalization).* The magnitude of a generalized response will decrease as the stimulus becomes more and more remote from the original conditioning stimulus.

Social habits and language are established by stimulus and response generalizations. Many symptoms are also the product of generalizations, phobias and paranoidal projections, for example. In transference one may observe the operation of generalization. During psychotherapy, the release of positive feelings and behavior in the relationship with the therapist will tend to generalize toward other interpersonal relationships. The corrective emotional experience of therapy thus extends itself into the arena of life.

It is important to emphasize again that many of the learning theories and the implications for psychotherapy deriving from them have been arrived at from work with lower animals. Man

---

* While there is no such thing as the "same" response, shades of difference always being present, for practical reasons they may be considered "similar."

operates on a level of organization that is unique to himself as a social and thinking creature possessed of the function of symbolic communication. Not all motives are reducible to organic needs, nor is tension reduction a completely adequate model for human motivation. A phenomenal representation of need states and end states is vital to a dynamic conception of learning. Goal achievement, as has been indicated in the previous chapter, involves cognitive structuring which activates behavior with the envisaging of new goals. Nevertheless some useful ideas may be extracted from the drive reduction theorists and adapted to certain phases of the psychotherapeutic process.

VIII

Psychoanalytic Theory

Freudian Approaches

MANY OF THE DISCOVERIES OF FREUD HAVE BEEN ACCEPTED AND incorporated with modifications into the different systems of psychotherapy. Among the most common are the following:

1. The principle of psychic determination.
2. The dynamic influence of the unconscious on everyday behavior.
3. The role of repression as a barrier to the unconscious.
4. The goal directed nature of all behavior.
5. The determining effect of psychosocial development on personality evolution, mechanisms of defense and the character structure.
6. The existence of sexual feelings and drives during childhood.
7. The contamination of adult behavior with immature needs and conflicts.
8. The impact on contemporary relationships of early forms of interaction with parental and sibling agencies (transference).
9. The central role of anxiety in sponsoring defensive operations, and symptom formation.
10. The understanding of symbolism.
11. The technique of free association.
12. The therapeutic impact of analyzing and interpreting resistance, transference and the transference neurosis.

1. Psychic determinism. The idea that mental processes are never fortuitous, but completely explicable in terms of certain antecedents is not new with Freud. The unique contribution of Freud was the establishment of causal connections for psychic events that seemingly had no purpose or meaning. More or less, psychic determinism has been accepted by the various schools of

78

psychological thought, although its spectrum has been widened by current neurophysiological investigations and the effects of the psychotropic drugs. The discovery that depression or schizophrenic disorganization may be activated by toxic substances and the products of faulty enzyme activities establishes more firmly the continuity of somatic and psychologic activities rather than the primacy of one over the other.

2. The unconscious.   Freud was not the discoverer of the ocean of the unconscious, but he was its chief navigator. The existence of mechanisms and structures functioning outside of awareness was known to writers and philosophers centuries before Freud; for instance, Herbert Carus, von Hartmann, Schopenhauer and Spinoza. Freud's contribution was to chart their extensions into everyday life, to demonstrate their dynamic operations and to indicate ways of detecting their content. The word "unconscious" has been repudiated by some authorities on the basis that it is verbally self-contradictory, that it confuses processes with underlying structures, and that it poses the paradox of a negative term connoting positive and dynamic properties. Some attempts have been made to substitute a more appropriate title like "non-reporting," "unverbalized," "unreflective," "conditioned signal;" however "unconscious" continues to be accepted as a collective name for a body of psychic operations that have either been expelled from the realm of awareness, or, in the form of primitive and infantile drives, have never reached its premises. Practically all systems of depth psychology acknowledge the existence of thoughts, feelings and impulses not immediately available to attention, but which nevertheless influence behavior. They attempt in therapy to elucidate on such processes, to remove resistances to their recognition, and to strengthen the inner resources of the individual to enhance his inner perceptions so that he may establish a clearer understanding of his motivational patterns. However, the specific warded off drives and conflicts that are considered basic,* the urgency of need to bring them forth, and the means by which this is accomplished will vary with the system.

---

* Freudian "oedipus complex," Adlerian "life style" and "festive aims," Rankian "birth trauma," Jungian "archtypes," etc.

3. Repression. The automatic banishing of certain psychic activities from awareness as a defense mechanism against anxiety, the mobilization by the patient of "resistances" of various kinds whenever unconscious content is approached, and the projection of the repudiated or prohibitive material into consciousness in the form of symbolic representations, are concepts generally accepted although language forms to describe this operative "censorship" are distinctive. Aspects of Freud's theories about repression are not completely accepted. For example, the idea of "primal repression," i.e., forbidden ingress to consciousness of certain instinctual processes (id activities), is not palatable to schools opposed to the instinct theory.

4. Goal directed nature of behavior. The demonstration by Freud that all behavior, even the most outlandish promptings and peculiar symptoms, are motivated toward specific objectives by inner needs (of which the individual may not be completely aware) is a doctrine that has gained wide acceptance. The kinds of motivations that propel the individual toward both rational and irrational activities are heterogenously identified by the different schools in terms of their particular orientations.

5. Psychosocial development. The tracing of symptoms to experiences in infancy and childhood led Freud to a longitudinal view of behavior, casting it in a historical perspective. He traced the sequence of change from birth onward biologically in terms of the vicissitudes of instincts (libido theory). His work encouraged an emerging developmental psychology which delineated characteristic behavior at various ages and stages of growth, described the course of development and the interaction of various developmental functions (see Piaget, Gesell, Erikson). The effect of focus on stages of development has been most constructive, even revolutionary. However, the terminologies and the explanations given by the Freudian school for behavior tendencies at different ages has served to promote controversy, accounting for many schisms in the analytic movement. Some authorities like Rado have retained a biologic theory, but have rejected the libido hypothesis. Others like Horney, Fromm, Sullivan and Kardiner have alleged that instinctual processes have little to do with the directions of personality, which is fashioned largely by value systems sustained in the ethos of a society. The most contentious point centers around the theory of infantile sexuality and its global application to stages of development.

6. Sexual promptings of childhood. Freud, in his explorations, uncovered the intense preoccupations of children with sexual feelings, sexual differences and birth processes, as well as the conflicts that these engrossments entailed. He demonstrated how sexual distortions survived in the unconscious, fostering perversions and symptomatic outcroppings in adult life. In his libido theory he presumed a broad conception of sexuality as encompassing both self-preservation and race preservation, insisting that its final race-preservative aim was the outgrowth of an instinctual development that employed early undifferentiated erogenous zones (mouth, anus, etc.). The energies of these zones were destined ultimately for final adult genital participation. Sexual instincts were thus presumed to be numerous, emanating from organic sources, bent upon attaining "organ pleasure," and acting at first independent of one another, only at later stages achieving synthesis in the function of reproduction. The extension of the term "sexuality" to infantile growth activities created much dissension among Freud's followers. Jung (1928) while acknowledging that much in the psyche depended on sex, protested that not all depended on it. Indeed other instincts, like self-preservation and self-assertion, could be dominant. Adler (1917) subordinated the sexual instinct to the feeling of inferiority which was mobilized by the desire for knowledge of sex differences and the uncertainty of one's sexual role. He considered the masculine protest against feminine promptings, and power impulses to be dominant. Later "neofreudian" rebels, including Horney, Fromm and Sullivan, revolted against Freud's conceptions of infantile sexuality. While the neofreudian group have acknowledged the presence of sexual interests and drives in childhood, they have differed from the Freudians in their interpretation of these promptings. They particularly denied that character formation issued out of stages of libido development; for example, collecting or miserliness as a manifestation of an anal-retentive phase. Social conditionings, they insisted, were of prime importance superceding biological factors and extending the boundaries of human potentialities that were circumscribed by the Freudian biological orientation which considered civilization itself a symbolic derivative of frustrated libidinal aims. Freud's pessimistic concepts of civilization, and the innate barbarous structure of man that dragooned him to violence, prejudice and destruction, has tended to alienate those persons who claim to subscribe to the inherent good of humans and their unlimited prospects for development. In their repudiation of this aspect of Freudian theory, nonconformists have sometimes minimized or discarded the entire body of his contributions, many of which they continue to accept and to employ under different tags with no acknowledgement of their source. In the Soviet Union, for example, Freudian ideas are considered unsound, yet a good number of psychoanalytic ideas and methods are utilized, wittingly or unwittingly by some Soviet psychiatrists who are quite dynamic in their approach.

The old nature-nurture polemic is particularly intense in regard to the purported nuclear complex of all neuroses, the oedipus complex, perhaps Freud's greatest treasure trove. The solution of this conflict, innate and universal, according to Freud, during which sexual energy shifted toward interest in the parents, determined the nature of the individual's later adjustments and particularly the character of his sexuality. While most professionals admit the presence of an oedipus complex and concede that it acts as a fertile source of neurotic difficulties, there is considerable disagreement regarding its origin and universality. There are those who contend that the oedipus complex is present only as a manifestation of operative neurotic processes in the child, originating in early infancy, the product of faulty parental handling, particularly overprotection and seduction. Under propitious circumstances then the child can escape the oedipal destiny. Yet some believe that our culture breeds the oedipus complex pervasively. Still others, while repudiating the libido theory and the concepts of pre-genital sexuality, contend that the oedipus complex is not experientially inspired; rather it is an innate phenomenon found in all people, its manifestations varying with the culture. As such it is capable of being modified and certain of its manifestations inhibited by social pressures. The problem of the oedipus complex is a burning one for neo-freudians who reject its ubiquity, since Freud

(1952) contended that no one had the right to call himself a psychoanalyst who did not accept the oedipus complex as the basic ingredient in neurosis.

Disagreement also exists among professionals regarding the traditional idea of a viable superego as the representative of society within the psyche that takes its final form as a reaction to the oedipus complex. Only then does it make itself felt as a mediator between the ego and the id. Some authorities believe that the superego precipitates prior to the oedipal period, even when it first arises on the bases of identification with some aspects of introjected parents. Doubt is cast on the accepted mechanism of superego formation during the oedipal period which holds that the sexual and murderous impulses from the id are permitted access to the ego during this phase, thus being withdrawn from their objects and placed in the ego, the changed portion of which becomes the superego. A part of the ego then contains the sadism toward the parent of the same sex and the love for the parent of the opposite sex; the introjection of the parent and the changing of the object libido to ego libido resulting in desexualization. The introjected objects fuse with the prephallic parental introjects and in this way the superego crystallizes. There are some observers like Melanie Klein (1958) who contend that supergo formation begins immediately after birth when the introjective process starts. Insisting that the innate oedipus complex manifests itself not at the accepted oedipal period, but during the last half of the first year of life, she has evolved the thesis, with the concordance of a considerable body of followers, that the superego precedes the appearance of the oedipus complex concurrent with the "depressive position." The infant projects feelings onto the mother's breast as "good" and "bad." The introjection of the "good" and "bad" breast is the structure around which the oedipus complex is said to be built. Her challenging of the Freudian mechanism of superego formation (which contends that identifications with the parents are the outcome of the oedipus complex and "only succeed if the oedipus complex is successfully overcome") has become one source of controversy in the analytic movement. A considerable amount of writing exists attempting to explain the mechanics of superego formation (Nunberg, 1944; Fenichel, 1945; Laforgue, 1940). Contrasting with these authorities are those who acknowledging the verity of many of Freud's ideas about infantile sexuality but insist that psychoanalytic theories of the formation of the ethical and moral self, the superego, are too complex and fanciful, drawing too much from mythology and speculation. They offer instead an explanation oriented around learning theory and conditioning.

Freud's concept of the "latency period," which follows the oedipal phase and precedes puberty, during which the sexual instinct is presumed to be dormant, has also come under criticism by many observers who contend that the dormancy, more imagined than real, is an aspect of the cultural repression of sexuality. They point to societies, which do not require of the child a sublimation of sexuality or a masking of its manifestations under nonreproductive activities, where open expressions of sexuality occur normally.

Irrespective of the disagreements among analysts and among non-analysts about the specific forms of sexuality that are present in childhood and the vicissitudes of the instincts entering into adult genitality, Freud opened the door to a neglected world. Many of his clinical observations regarding the concern of children during the first years of life with the processes of reproduction and birth, genital differences, fears of castration, with accompanying denial mechanisms (penis envy in girls, phallic conceptions of women in boys) and sexual attachments to their parents are popularly accepted as constituting prevailing patterns of behavior in all children. A tolerance of childhood sexual curiosities and practices, and institution of measures of sexual education, have led to a more wholesome management of a conventionally taboo subject. Freud's observations about the primal scene, oedipus complex, and distortions of the sexual drive as registered in inhibitions, perversions and exaggerations have had a profound effect in clarifying mystifying psychopathological phenomena, although his theories explaining their origin have not been accepted in their totality.

7. **Persistence of early conditionings.** Freud's confirmation of Haeckel's hypothesis that ontogeny recapitulates phylogeny, in that man in his own development rehearses his ancestral experiences (a mnemonic echo of "father of the primal horde") has not gained general acceptance, although Jung expanded this proposi-

tion in his doctrine of "archetypes" alluding to the determining role of racial elements in the human psyche. Freud's fundamental contribution was to demonstrate the historical ferment operating in personality development, and to show that while broad aspects of personality were fashioned in the template of biology, the lines along which it evolved were conditioned by the culture. It is indeed impossible to understand character structure and symptom formation without referring to the formative experiences of childhood. Surviving in almost pristine form are residues of these experiences as unpropitiated needs which enjoin the individual: (1) to seek childish gratifications which may pervert an adult adjustment; (2) to indulge coping mechanisms and defenses which, useful once in handling childish anxieties, may no longer have a functional utility; and (3) to repeat ("repetition–compulsion") in an irrational way, a kind of futile reliving of early emotional experiences which have no potentiality for pleasure. While Freud's explanations for these processes may not be concurred with by some, his emphasis of their determining effect on adult behavior is widely acknowledged.

8. Transferential reactions. Of vital importance to psychotherapists of all persuasions is Freud's crucial perception that to a greater or lesser degree patients tend to project onto authority figures thoughts, wishes and feelings identical to those harbored toward important personages (parents, parental substitutes, siblings) in their past. Reanimated during therapy are reactions, wholly inappropriate for the present, but which recapitulate important emotional situations in the past. It is as if the patient seeks to relive his infancy and childhood, recovering vital gratifications through the instrumentality of a new relationship in which the therapist is endowed with magical powers and a supreme omniscience, such as an infant harbors toward parental agencies. There may be exhibited also toward him a host of other aberrant attitudes, such as rebelliousness, hostility, submissiveness and sexual excitement. Such transference feelings may also develop outside of the therapeutic situation, with any kind of an authority or sibling figure. The diagnostic importance of the transference phenomenon is obvious, since it is a laboratory revival of much of what went on in the individual's childhood.

9. Anxiety and mechanisms of defense. The function of anxiety in promoting the various mechanisms of defense and in provoking symptom formation is generally accepted as one of the principal contributions of Freud. Originally Freud conceived of anxiety as a transformation of libido which could otherwise not be discharged. He revised this notion later specifically designating anxiety as a response of the ego to the overwhelming influx of stimuli, external or internal, too powerful to be mastered or discharged. It especially developed from pressure of instinctual demands prohibited by reality or forbidden by the superego (id anxiety). Anxiety, differentiated from fear (the reaction to a real danger) could register itself as a conscious perception (anxiety reaction) or as a disrupted physiological state (anxiety equivalent). Consciously recognized it could be "free floating," attaching itself indiscriminately to any situation or activity (anxiety neurosis) or it could be displaced and projected onto symbols representative of the repressed conflict (anxiety hysteria). Early in life the child learns to respond to the *signal* of anxiety, reacting to the possibility of anxiety before it gets out of hand. A series of typical danger situations confront every child which set off the anxiety signal: (1) fear of separation from the mother during the first year ("primal anxiety," "separation anxiety," "fear of the loss of the love object"); (2) fear of the loss of love from the parent during the second year; (3) castration fears from $2\frac{1}{2}$ to 5; and (d) guilt and fear of disapproval from the superego after 5 or 6. Such situations with an anxiety potential remain in the unconscious throughout life. Mechanisms of defense are developed by the ego to deal with the threat of anxiety, and to avert guilt, disgust, shame and other responses of the superego. Among such defenses, elaborated by Freud and his followers, are regression, introjection, repression, projection, reaction formation, isolation, undoing, displacement, rationalization, sublimation, denial, reversal, turning against the self, postponement of affects, affect equivalents, change in quality of affects, displacement of instinctual aims, condensation, and symbolization (Freud, A., 1948; Fenichel, 1945; Hinsie, 1940).

Freud's concepts about the central role of anxiety and the defensive operations to control its manifestations are acknowledged as vital to an understanding of dynamic psychiatry and psychopathology, although shifts in emphasis, and unique elaborations and explanations of the mechanism of anxiety are often in terms other than those phrased by Freud.

10. Symbolism.   The pivotal elaborations by Freud of the role of symbolism in the mental life of the individual are well known and accepted by most schools. To avoid censorship and thus avert anxiety a disguised conscious representation of unconscious prohibited drives is indulged, the individual generally being unaware of the substitution or displacement. Abstract and complex ideas may thus be represented in sensorial and concrete terms; the specific kinds of representation commonly drawing from primitive language forms in which oral, excretory and phallic components are prominent. Sexual symbols, actual or disguised, particularly portray incorporation, gratification, punishment, power, humiliation and annihilation meanings. Symbolism is the language of dreams and of psychiatric symptoms, and its understanding gives the therapist clues to inner wishes and conflicts. Thus a fear of snakes or daggers may be a symbol for a wish for a penis or for penal penetration. A fear of being bitten by animals may disguise an infantile impulse to devour the mother or her breast. Delusions, hallucinations, obsessions, compulsions, phobias, hysterical conversions, morbid affects, hypochondrias and the personalization of organs and organ systems are explicable only by considering their symbolic connotations. Projective tests, employing unstructured materials, are instituted on the translation of symbols. The structure, function and therapeutic employment of symbolism in dreams are among Freud's greatest contributions to the psychological field.

Freud pointed out the regressive archaic quality of symbolism, the language of dreams; for instance, the kinship to the style of ancient mankind and processes of primitive thought, ideas later expanded by Jung. The phylogenic origin of symbols, and the existence of universal symbolism are not so completely accepted as is the general idea that symbolism is an unconscious process, developed during the lifetime of the individual, organized around association and similarity whereby one object comes to represent another object through some quality or aspect the two have in common.

11. Free association. Freud's disclosure that unguided and unconstrained verbalizations penetrated into unconscious zones and revealed warded off content is considered a most significant means of understanding inner conflict, as well as of encouraging the eventual development of a transference neurosis in the event such a contingency is deemed therapeutically important. Lifting restraints on censorship, thus sidetracking repression, provide fruitful guides to underlying motivations and dynamics. Interpretation of the patient's unguarded spontaneous utterances, or abandoned thoughts related to dreams, phantasies and slips of speech, establish vital connections with and understanding of unconscious drives and conflicts. While free association is employed as the preferred type of communication in classical Freudian psychoanalysis, it has a utility as an instrument for delving into unconscious aspects of mental operations in other forms of insight therapy. To expedite the uncovering of unconscious material various schools employ the Freudian techniques of free association, and the interpretation of resistance and transference in a relatively objective, passive, nonevaluating setting, although active and unique measures are sometimes introduced to expedite or to modulate these techniques.

12. Analysis of resistance and transference. Freud contended that cure depended upon the releasing from the unconscious of repudiated and repressed infantile and primitive longings into consciousness where they could be examined and understood. This was accomplished best where the patient was helped by the therapist to an awareness of his defensive resistances, many of which were imbedded in his character structure, and that shielded him from an acknowledgement of his drives and conflicts.

Insight therapies which aim at the reconstructing of personality employ many of Freud's tactics to detect and remove resistances. This is considered necessary due to an inevitable struggle between forces that support the illness and those that help the ego to give it up, i.e., the work of the therapist. Resistances, however, are myriad, subtle and ingenious. The therapist must deal with *conscious resistances* in the form of the intentional withholding of information, the breaking of appointments, attempts at seduction and engaging in a battle of wits. More important are *unconscious resistances* mobilized by anxiety at the return of the repressed elements such as silence in "transference resistance" with unrealistic feelings being projected onto the therapist in a refusal to relinquish the illness gain. Such manifestations ward off anxiety and subversively serve as a means of gratifying repudiated needs, in a persistent repetition-compulsion of early self-defeating experiences, and in a pervasive need for punishment issuing out of a sense of guilt. Of special importance are *transference resistances* in which feelings for parents or important siblings are released in the relationship and then repressed. Resistance emerges when probings are attempted, often eventuating in conflict and expressed forcefully in negative feelings and attitudes toward the therapist. Non-insight therapies are also sabotaged by the occurrence of resistance, and an understanding of resistance and a knowledge of when and how to manage it by interpretation have proven helpful to therapists, many of whom have rejected Freud's instinctual formulations.

Of significance in formal psychoanalysis is the development and working through of a *transference neurosis* considered by many as Freud's most important therapeutic discovery. This manifestation, deliberately provoked by certain tactics on the part of the analyst, is characterized by the lighting up of an infantile neurosis, an aspect of the oedipus complex, and its projection into the therapeutic situation; the analyst being regarded as if he were one or both parents toward whom sexual and hostile feelings explode. This artificial neurosis lights up incest prohibitions and destructive ego attitudes that have been sealed off in the unconscious, opportunity then being afforded the patient to overcome the infantile neurosis that is sustaining his present difficulty, in a more tolerant, protected and understanding setting. While the formal psychoanalytic technique is limited in its practical application, and while many patients are not suited as candidates for this procedure, it offers, where it is indicated and where the therapist knows how to employ it, the greatest opportunity for reconstructive personality change. Even though a transference neurosis is not employed as a therapeutic tool, its understanding is important for the therapist who deals with patients on any kind of relationship level, if no more than to circumvent it when without design it begins to emerge.

Ego Analytic Approaches

Basic contributions of the "Ego Analysts" are these:

1. Behavior is determined by forces other than instinct in the form of response sequences encompassed under the classification of "ego."

2. The ego as an entity has an autonomy separate from both instinct and reality.

3. The ego supports drives for environmental mastery and adaptive learning which are divorced from sexual and aggressive instincts.

4. The adaptive aspects of learned behavior are as important as instinctual behavior and lead to important gratifications in their own right.

5. A greater emphasis must be put on the environment and on healthy, as opposed to pathologic, behavior than in orthodox Freudian approaches. An understanding of pathological behavior in relation to normal behavior is vital.

6. Personality is more plastic and modifiable, even beyond the period of childhood, than is traditionally supposed. A more hopeful prognosis is consequently forecast.

7. The human being is the master of his destiny who can control and select his behavioral patterns to achieve differentiated goals.

8. Society is a force that does not necessarily emerge from man's expressions of instinct; nor does it always thwart the biological nature of man. It can exert a constructive influence on him while modifying primitive instinctual drives.

9. Conscious and learned responses are basic to man's adjustment.

10. Technical innovations in the direction of greater activity are sometimes necessary.

The conviction that human behavior is too complex to be accounted for purely in terms of instinctual processes has turned a body of Freudians toward the focal consideration of other dimensions of personality than the id, particularly the ego, while retaining fidelity to the dynamic, structural, economic, topographic and other basic psychoanalytic concepts, including the libido theory. Among the first of these "ego analysts" were Anna Freud

(1946), Hartmann (1950, 1951, 1958), Rapaport (1950, 1958, 1960, 1961), Kris (1951), Lowenstein (1953), and Erikson (1946, 1950). The direction of the ego analysts has been less introspective and speculative than it has been empirical, based on factual investigations, the systematic gathering of data and organized experiment. Attempts have been made to avoid philosophical issues and implications in order to deal more scientifically with facts. This has led to an intensive study of the child and his responses to various child rearing practices, of interactions within the family, as well as the influence of the community. Sociological and anthropological vectors have accordingly entered into some of the emerging formulations, although the orientation is definitely a biological one.

While primary psychological drives are considered basic and important these are dealt within the context of the molding and modifying influence of environment which is believed to play a decisive role in eliciting behavior independent of instinctual forces. Building on Freud's conceptions of instinct, ego analysts regard behavior as undifferentiated at birth, the infant possessing certain response potentials, innately derived, but requiring the influence of environment to arouse and consolidate them into adaptive sequences. Among the groupings of responses are certain internal and external elicitors of behavior which are distinctive from instincts, those that deal with responses to perceptual stimuli and those that serve organizing, integrating and controlling functions. Response patterns serve to adjust the individual to his particular environment. Innately determined also are other responses such as awareness and thought which serve to control and to direct behavior. Learned responses soon displace instinctual and automatic reactions. Behavior is more than a means of reduction of sexual and aggressive energies. Ego functions can be pleasurable in their own right. Among the most important ego functions are those that mediate perception and sensation and support operations that maintain contact with the external and internal environment; there are those that deal with awareness and attention, and can help delay or inhibit impulses; those that govern thinking and communicating (verbal response); and others that control action and motility, enabling the individual to manage his environment. The ego in its synthetic, integrating and organizing operations fosters a controlled, thoughtful, planned, and efficient mediation of behavior directed at consciously selected goals.

While psychosocial development is crucial during the first five years of life, laying down as it does the patterns that will determine the individual's behavior the remainder of his existence, these patterns are not as completely fixed and unmodifiable as the earlier Freudian theorists supposed. Nevertheless, at certain stages of growth environmental experiences can have a decisive influence on the total personality structure.

Ego development occurs immediately after birth as the child discriminates between his inner responses and the influences of his environment, for instance, in feeding. Gradually the child comes to differentiate himself from the environment, and to anticipate future events. Frustrations encourage self-control. The child develops the ability to recall past situations where delay in gratification was followed by fulfillment. Habitual response patterns are developed in relationship to objects around him which enable him to win their approval and to control his feelings from within. A sense of personal continuity and identity emerge. Problem solving and coping are aided by imitation (identification). The social milieu becomes incorporated within the individual seducing the child, as Erikson has put it, to its particular life style. Self-esteem is built from exercise of different skills and the fulfilling of interpersonal experiences. Defense mechanisms are evolved to control fear and the situations to which it becomes conditioned. The signal of anxiety serves to mobilize defenses in the repertoire of the child and, although the early conditions that fostered them no longer exist, the individual may continue to employ them throughout his life. Learned patterns of behavior establish themselves as "hierarchial structures" from the base of the earliest patterns to the apex of the latest responses, the original ones never being completely ablated but merely replaced by the later ones. This applies also to thoughts, at the foundation of which are primitive "primary process" thought patterns concerned with instinctual drive reduction replaced gradually by logical thought. Furthermore the mechanisms of defense are in hierarchial arrangements. Their antecedents reside in physiological responses and their latest representations are in the form of creative thought.

Behavior is considered as neither the by-product of instinctual energies, nor the result of situational events. Rather it is a mode that reflects and yet gradually achieves relative independence from both through the development of autonomous stable response structures. Healthy behavior is under conscious control. Where the ego loses its autonomy from the id or from reality, behavior is no longer under conscious control and pathology may ensue. This is particularly the case where residual stable behavior patterns are insufficient to deal with an existing stress situation. A variety of circumstances contribute to the formation and maintenance of learned adaptive structures and a consideration of these is vital to the understanding of behavior pathology.

In therapy, which is conducted under orthodox Freudian rules, an added goal is an attempt at expansion of the repertoire of learned patterns to enhance conscious control of behavior in relation to both inner impulses and environmental pressures. Hartmann has speculated that eventually a technique system would be evolved that can keep abreast of new theoretical developments. Under such a system an effort would be made to understand not only pathological, but adaptive behavior patterns and to examine the interrelationship between the conflict and nonconflict aspects of the ego while tracing the antecedants of neurotic anxiety. There is an implication in some of the writings of ego analysts that therapy should embody more active procedures than in the orthodox technique. For instance, interpretations should be couched in terms of specific events rather than in abstract concepts.

Neo-Freudian Approaches

Among the contributions of the neo-freudians are the following propositions:

1. Personality is fashioned principally by cultural rather than instinctual forces; the value systems of society are incorporated in the individual's character structure and determine his action tendencies; conflict is a product of diverse factors within and outside of the person and involves both conscious and unconscious factors.

2. The myriad elements—social, interpersonal, intrapsychic— entering into the character organization necessitates a comprehen-

sive and holistic viewpoint in personality theory, and a concern with healthy as well as abnormal adaptation.

3. The libido theory and death instinct theory are formulations that cannot explain either normal or abnormal behavior; infantile sexuality alone cannot account for man's basic conflicts or for the lines along which his character structure develops.

4. Female sexuality is an entity on a parity with, rather than inferior to, male sexuality.

5. The therapeutic encounter is more than a means of repeating and working through early traumatic experiences; it is an experience in relationship containing positive growth potentials that can lead to greater self-actualization.

6. Activity and flexibility in therapeutic approach are essential; this encourages eclecticism in method.

7. An optimistic rather than pessimistic viewpoint is justified regarding man's potentials as a creative, loving and peaceful being.

1. Primacy of cultural factors in personality development. Following the original lead of Alfred Adler, and stressing concepts from field theory, neo-freudians regard the environment not as a projection vehicle molded by instinctual needs and demands, but rather as the cardinal force in its own right that shapes personality. Behavior is conceived of as the product of many vectors, biological and social. Constitutional and hereditary elements while present do not determine man's destiny. This is mediated principally by experiences in life. Attention must, therefore, be focused not on the unconscious, on instincts and their vicissitudes, but on the relationship of the individual with the significant personages in his early and later development who are carriers of the value systems of the culture. Personal values reflect these systems. Distortions in relationships and in values are registered in the character structure, disparate operations of which act as a potent source of conflict. While there is general agreement among the various neo-freudian groups with these ideas, the most important cultural determinants, the specific effects that are registered on character structure, and the consequences of such impacts are discrepant. The existence, the role and the contents of the unconscious are also matters about which there is disagreement.

2. The holistic viewpoint in abnormal and healthy adaptation.
The concept of character as fashioned by the culture has directed
attention to the institutions and values of society that foster
healthy and unhealthy adaptation. Instead of viewing healthy
aspects of personality through the lens of pathological distortions,
neo-freudians have tended to investigate what goes on in the
"normal" or healthy individual, drawing inferences from data
dealing with adaptive rather than sick behavior. Abnormal behavior is considered in the framework of understanding of the
"normal" rather than the reverse. This has widened the horizons
of progressive personality research to pertinent areas of sociology,
social psychology, ecology, anthropology, ethology and philosophy.
The focus of inquiry is on the intricate network of organizational
units, interpersonal, familial, group, national and international as
well as the sum total of institutions that constitute society as a
whole. Behavioral studies are encouraged that scrutinize the
interaction of individuals and groups in a variety of settings. The
habits, manners, mores and customs of men in primitive and
civilized organizations are surveyed and cross cultural data on
child rearing practices analyzed. Modes of reacting to aspects of
the environment that constitute the individual's life space, and
ecological patterns of such phenomena as crime, delinquency,
poverty and insanity are examined. The behavior of animals in
their natural habitat is observed to determine the relative roles of
instincts and of social learning. Finally, studies of aesthetic, moral,
ethical and spiritual promptings, of social values and how they are
internalized and influence behavior, bring the behavioral scientist
into the fields of philosophy and religion. Scientists from diverse
fields cooperating together in interdisciplinary research foster a
better integration of the biological and social sciences. By considering the human being in totality, neo-freudian approaches
support a holistic and Gestalt point of view. The individual is
considered a tapestry of biochemical, physiological, psychological,
sociological and spiritual systems, with a feedback of each of these
systems onto the others.

3. Shortcomings of the instinct theory. The libido theory as
a developmental as well as therapeutic model, ingenious as it is, is
considered by neo-freudians to be inadequate in explaining what

goes on in all personality operations. It is believed to be highly over-generalized extending itself into zones of energy exchange which cannot possibly deal with the complexities of human relationships. For instance, pregenital instinctual drives are not the basic elements involved in character organization. On the other hand, parental attitudes and practices do have a determining effect upon feeding, excretory, assertive, aggressive, and sexual patterns—indeed, a greater impact than forces of maturation. Experiences in the family are the cradle of faulty conditionings. Personality functions are best conceived of in an interactional or transactional framework. This calls for a different perspective on such phenomena as infantile sexuality. All bodily activities should not be regarded as adumbrations of sexuality. For instance, pleasure in feeding and excreting cannot conceivably be sexual even in the broadest sense of the word. Evidence of the sexualization of certain bodily activities during analysis does not necessarily prove the case for pansexual development in childhood. Even frank genital exploration and manipulation in childhood may be less a sign of true sexuality than a mark of curiosity and the seeking of knowledge of how the body is constituted. Where childhood sexual aberrancies develop and persist, this is evidence of a disturbed upbringing, of precocious erotic stimulation, and of response to anxiety rather than of anarchial sexual instincts.

The presence of the oedipus complex during psychosocial development is not disputed, but its universality and ultimate destiny are questioned. Some neo-freudians accept firmly the ubiquitous biological nature of the oedipus complex, but contend that its form is influenced by the particular culture in which the child is reared. Others believe that the oedipus complex is not a biological phenomenon, but rather the product of provocative conditionings particularly in families which encourage strong dependent attitudes in children or in which the child encounters excessive sexual stimulation through the over-fondling activities of the parents. Cultures where such dependency or sexually seductive attitudes do not exist, do not foster the oedipus complex in children. Where the oedipus complex develops, it may be a manifestation of discord and distrust between the parents resulting in their utilizing the child as a vehicle for frustrated love needs. The emotions of jealousy and hostility in the child emerge as a by-product of the conflict that is engendered in him. The child selects the "strong" and dominant parent—mother or father—as an identification vehicle, and, where mothers play the dominant role, the child will for security's sake tend to identify with the mother. This can create problems in sexual identification for the boy. The oedipus complex may accordingly be understood in cultural terms as a reaction to anxiety, and not necessarily as a manifestation of the libido.

The death instinct is also labeled a metaphysical concept rather than a plausible theory to account for aggression, masochism and sadism. It has little theoretical or clinical usefulness. Aggression is not a primary drive, but a secondary reaction to frustration. Masochism is a special kind of defensive response to anxiety marshalled by certain interpersonal conflicts.

Dualistic formulations regarding sexuality and aggressiveness are not considered adequate in explaining the complexity of these drives. For instance, bisexuality is not universal as some authorities insist. Though rudiments physically of the opposite sex are present in an individual, this does not justify the notion that they must influence his mental life (Lillie, 1931; Rado, 1956). The idea of universal latent homosexuality has led to therapeutic nihilism in treating homosexual problems. Placing a higher biologic value on the aggressive quality of the male genital is also unjustified; the crediting of superiority to the penis as compared to the female genital being a cultural phenomenon that can easily shift with a change in social values.

4. A positive approach to female psychology. Male oriented concepts of female psychology which regard women as arrested males, frustrated by their biological inferiority, are alleged to be a product of the cultural consideration of women as an inferior species. Under these circumstances penis envy when it develops is a manifestation of the underdog philosophy foisted on females by the dominant males. By possessing a fantasied penis and through masculine strivings a woman compensates for her feelings of social inferiority. Similarly, assigning passivity, dependency and masochism as female characterics does not reveal their true non-sexual dynamic qualities. Female psychology, therefore, can be explained purely in cultural rather than biological terms. On the other hand, there are biological differences between males and females, and there are variant social roles they must assume. For instance, motherhood imposes certain demands on women that makes for characteristics distinctive from those of males.

5. Fallacy of classical topography. Bounding mental activity, the topographic conception of the mental apparatus in terms of superego, ego and id is not believed to be adequate for the explanation of psychic functions. Overweighting of the superego and id in conventional analytic formulations has left the ego a barren area. Moreover breathing life into the id-ego-superego trinity, giving them substance and location, and charging them with human lusts, fears, hostilities and jealousies, are both animistic and clinically untenable. The id is not the core of all human energy and activity. The concept of the superego is a confusing one since it incorporates both the healthy elements of the conscience and neurotic, compulsive qualities. The values embraced by the supergo are not a mere facsimile of standards incorporated from parental agencies, but reflect a variety of other conditionings in addition.

6. The therapeutic encounter as a positive growth experience. The therapeutic relationship is a two-way transaction in which a feedback of feeling issues between therapist and patient. What is effective in therapy is not the expulsion from the unconscious of material that results in startling insights, but the emotional experience of two individuals relating to each other in a productive way. The therapeutic interpersonal relationship has a healing effect that mobilizes the patient's capacities in the solution of his own problems. The therapist is never neutral during this process. His values and prejudices filter through irrespective of how much he tries to act as a neutral screen. His nonverbal responses, the emphasis on certain kinds of content, and the nature of his interpretations all reflect his personal standards that will influence the lines along which the patient thinks, the kinds of ideas he will retain, and the direction he will follow in revising his life style. This has led to a deliberate abandonment of anonymity on the part of the neo-freudian analyst, a release of his interpersonal spontaneity, the ability to reveal personal values which are proffered as potential contingencies rather than as absolute mandates. Expression of hostility in the patient during analysis is not necessarily an index of good therapy marking release of repressed, transferential energy. It may be a manifestation of provocations inspired by the therapist's rejecting and detached attitude. Aggression is regarded as a secondary reaction to frustration and as a defense against anxiety. When it occurs in therapy, it is usually being mobilized as a response to conflict within the immediate interpersonal relationship. Rather than helping, it may be a detriment to therapeutic progress. There is a tendency among neo-freudians to consider conscious aspects of experience as important, if not more important, than unconscious operations in the formation of conflict. Indeed some neo-freudians depreciate the value of probings into unconscious ideation.

7. **"Eclecticism" in therapeutic method.** The realization that most patients cannot avail themselves of the opportunity of coming to sessions four to six times weekly, and that of those who can do so, many are unsuited for intensive probing and the rigors of a transference neurosis, has led to a reduction in the number of sessions and to greater activity and flexibility in the therapist's tactics, relaxation of the fundamental rule of free association, and the introduction of a variety of adjunctive procedures within the framework of treatment. Without arguing the points as to whether such stratagems convert the gold of psychoanalysis into a baser metal, whether results of this "eclecticism" are more superficial being based on suggestion, whether reconstruction of personality is by-passed in favor of symptom relief and the expediency of environmental adjustment, the amalgam has proven helpful to larger numbers of patients than could have been reached by orthodox techniques.

8. **A constructive philosophy toward man.** In minimizing the fixity of behavior in instincts, a different philosophy toward man is encouraged. He is more than an animal whose biological heritage chains him to the limitations of his inner strivings. He is not basically lecherous or destructive. These characteristics, if they

occur, are environmentally nurtured. Emphasis on the essential goodness of mankind, not as a reaction formation to aggressive and destructive instincts, but as a quality in its own right emphasizes positive values as determining forces in the creation and molding of personality. It substantiates the human being as a creature who has needs to receive and to extend "tenderness," "care" and "love" for others.

IX

Social Theory; Role Theory; Group Dynamics

WHILE ADMITTING THE UTILITY OF EVOLUTIONARY AND DRIVE theory, and accepting the presence of innate fixed motor patterns in man, a basic assumption, entertained by the majority of social scientists, is that the transmission agencies of behavioral tendencies are not the genes, but rather parental authorities, who, through discipline and education, impound the value systems of society on the child. Man, then, is the product both of a physiological heritage passed on to him through his genes, and of a cultural heritage which he imbibes through the processes of identification and learning.

Investigations of how this learning comes about have concerned sociologists, social psychologists and anthropologists (Durkheim, 1915; Cooley, 1922; Malinowsky, 1929; Benedict, 1934; Mead, 1934; Kardiner, 1939). Studies of the evolution of the self and the role of language in relation to others clearly indicate how society gives shape to the developing awareness of the person's own existence (G. Mead, 1934). The application of experimental method to the techniques of the social sciences has gradually resulted in explorations of the individual quantitatively as part of the group, while maintaining an objectivistic, behavioral viewpoint toward the data observed in social interaction (Allport, 1924). For instance, experimental work with perceptual processes demonstrates how social perception evolves with the establishing of unifying group norms and group goals which replace discordant individual judgments and perceptions (Sherif, 1935). Models for sociological research have included sociometric techniques (Moreno, 1934), and methods for the analysis of field forces and group dynamics as they impinge on the individual as in social–stress and leader-follower situations (Lewin, 1935).

101

Incentives for sociological research are contained in the substantive realization that the human being, from birth on, is dependent for his survival upon the social group. How he develops, thinks, feels and behaves can be understood only as part of group life. The ordinances of society—its institutions, cultures, ideologies and stratifications—operate uninterruptedly. The domestication of family, the assignments of education, the indoctrinations of religion, the pressures of economics, the burdens of bureaucracy and the force of government all impinge on the individual, manipulating and molding his characterologic contours. Clinicians implicate social forces as prime precipitating agencies in emotional illness. Among such forces are instrumentalities operative during the ontological development of the individual, such as inadequate mothering, improper disciplining, severe strife within the family, the absence of a parental model, substandard living conditions, a pathological neighborhood and any other external factors that deprive the person of opportunities for appropriate need gratification, stimulation and learning. In adult life many conflictual determinants encompass the individual as a result of the variant role relationships pursued with other human beings, as well as his stressful daily interactions with diverse social institutions. Thus any environmental situation that deprives the individual of security, devalues his self-esteem and robs him of the opportunities for creative self-fulfillment will act as a source of psychological strain.

An understanding of social factors, including the contemporary research findings in the field, is vital for the psychotherapist since many of the schools of psychotherapy have been crucially influenced by the work of sociologists and social psychologists, both in theories of human behavior and conflict, and in techniques of control and treatment. Of particular interest are data related to social stratification, role theory and group dynamics.

Social Stratification

One of the most thoroughly investigated phenomena is that of social stratification. Determinated by such rational factors as education, experience and skills, stratification acts as a motivant to the "bettering of oneself" in societies where classes are mobile. Class immobility, however, as occurs in some societies, which makes it impossible to break through barriers for the proper reward of achievements and creativity, encourages hopelessness, defeat, resentment and depression. Stratification along the lines of caste is even more provocative since it labels groups as "superior" or "inferior" according to race, lineage, place of birth, and religious background, for which the individual is not responsible and over which he has no means of control. Where membership in a sacred superior circle carries with it power, privilege, status and economic opportunity, envy, resentment and fear in the out-group are inevitable, countered by the arrogant in-group assumption of divine right which is staunchly defended when challenged by various tactics, including violence. Clusters of subcultural groups stratify themselves in every society, each possessing its "norms" in the form of cherished mores, ideologies, folkways, ethics and linguistic differences. Distinctions may be detected among stratified groups in "norms" related to child rearing practices, such as toilet training, disciplining and management of sexual behavior, which leads to rigid attitudes and traits in adult life. Conflict of opposing values and ideologies among the different classes, castes and subcultural groups are bound to reflect themselves in individual and group pathology.

Role Theory

Society is an aggregate of persons with common goals whose positions enjoin them to assume specialized roles. The individual, constituted as he is with values, traits and attitudes (his "self"), develops action systems as a result of the interplay of self and role. Role theory deals with reciprocal relationships that go on between people. It also embraces the interaction of self and role. It contemplates personality as a tapestry of role behavior, of role perception and self-perception in the matrix of role (Murphy, 1947)).

The conventional definition of role as employed by G. Mead (1934) regards it as the pattern of attitudes and actions an individual exhibits in social situations. This is molded by his status or position in the social structure which obliges him to behave in certain ways. Special actions are expected of persons occupying certain roles ("role expectations") which meet some need in the social system (Parsons and Shils, 1951). The individual consequently organizes his behavior to fulfill his role expectations. Thus the student assumes with the teacher the role of learner; the teacher the role of educator. Roles are more or less implicit, being prescribed by the culture. The child learns that he is under set circumstances expected to behave in certain ways. Conformity brings rewards; revolt results in punishment. The little boy finds that his roles in society, his privileges and liberties, differ from those of a little girl. As he matures, his role expectations and behavior change. Juveniles, adolescents and adults perform differently both through intentional instruction and through incidental learning (Sarbin, 1959).

Ambiguous role expectations lead to conflict and to socially invalid role enactments. For example, many women in our culture, tending to equate some aspects of the feminine role with inferiority, resist complying with certain role expectations. Indeed they may seek a solution to their conflict by assuming a masculine role in some areas of adjustment. Role conflicts are, in such instances, inevitable. To some extent role conflicts encompass all human beings, since in certain areas of functioning every individual occupies two or more positions simultaneously and is unable to live up to all of his role expectations. The degree of role conflict and the inability of the individual to evolve adequate defenses to the dilemmas posed by his ambivalencies will determine their pathogenicity.

The role an individual believes he must play in a social context is a product of his perceptual and conceptual fields, which involve his past experiences and embrace many intrapsychic processes. The overt factors of role perception, for instance the acts and appearance of others, are colored and even distorted by internal needs and conflicts. Thus, where excessive dependency is a lingering impulse not resolved in the courses of maturation, the individual will implicitly assume the role of child with any person whom he perceives as an actual or potential parental substitute. The specific position assigned to the parental symbol will be that of authority. Where the symbol does not come up to the demanded role expectation of being and acting as the authority, conflict may ensue.

Though the unconscious is not acknowledged by some role theorists, its operations are present, prompting motivations that dragoon the individual to act out roles in opposition to traditional role expectations. Role enactment then may not validate the expectations of the person or persons with whom the individual is relating. This can give rise to conflict leading to mutual retaliation and other defenses. Multiple roles are the rule, the richer the repertoire of role potential, the more flexible and integrated the individual (Gough, 1948; Cameron and Margaret, 1951).

Role theorists regard the self as an intervening variable which can be approached through role concepts. The elusive entity of the self is an aspect of the total cognitive organization, an inference derived from interaction with other persons, objects and events. The self evolves as an organization of qualities, the resultant of maturational and personal-social experiences. Its formation is involved with the principle of the need for "constancy"—homeostasis—in the child, obtained by invoking the aid and intervention of other individuals around him. Awareness by the child of the "somatic self" that embraces tensions is the basis of the differentiation of self from non-self. External events become associated with tension reduction and the child's perception that certain motor activities on his part in relation to others lead to events which eliminate his tension, will act as further support for the foundation of self. Toward the end of the first year, a new cognitive structure is laid down in the form of gestures and other forms of communication which enables him to differentiate persons and objects from the acts of persons. At the same time there is discrimination between self-acts that are approved or disapproved. Perceiving, identifying and conceptualizing of roles and role expectations are elaborated as the child's symbolic development expands. The self-concept in role theory is thus intricately related to the socialization process and to the factor of reciprocal role playing with many significant persons. Out of such interactions there evolves the "social self." Difficulties in development result in "fixations" of the self concept on primitive or less mature levels than the "social self."

An interesting finding issuing from psychoanalysis that relates to the development of role expectations is that the child will divine, by uncanny perception, the verbally unexpressed but nevertheless obvious unconscious designs of the parent with whom he identifies himself. He will act out, either as a child or later in life, some of the unconscious parental needs and demands. Antisocial tendencies are often a reflection of the unconscious urges of parents, who, in their eagerness to conceal these promptings, give them undue emphasis in the form of warnings, reaction formations, defenses and symbolized expressions of repudiated drives (Szureck and Johnson, 1952). The parent may also confuse the child as to roles by alternately encouraging (seducing) and punishing (rejecting) him.

Harmony between the self and role enactment is one of the measures of adaptation. Performances to satisfy role expectations that are incongruent with the self (self-role conflicts), or two or more role expectations that clash with one another (role-role conflicts), will interfere with adjustment. Ego defense mechanisms are elaborated to reconcile such differences, and to maintain a constancy of the self in the face of expressing such discordant role expectations. Many self-maintaining mechanisms, such as the evolvement of a rationalizing philosophy, are implemented to support incongruent roles which are regarded as essential for adjustment. Where self-maintaining mechanisms fail, neurotic defenses may be exploited to bolster the self. If "constancy" (homeostasis) is still precarious, autistic and desocialized role enactment may come about. Where two or more roles are incompatible, and institutionalized forms are not available to reconcile opposing role enactments, conflicts may also ensue with eventuating defensive and disorganizing tendencies.

Group Dynamics

Man is a group animal expressing his most elemental as well as urbane needs through his relationships with other human beings. As part of a cluster, man is subject to many demands and pressures imposed on him by the group at the same time that he extracts from it his personal tokens and contributes to it his idiosyncratic offerings. *What* he does and *how* he relates to the group, and what in turn the group does to him and the other members, are subjects of concern to the behavioral scientist. Description of the observable variables in a group and delineation of the dynamics of interaction are the contributions of the field now known as "group dynamics." This field is distinctive from that of "personality dynamics," of which psychoanalysis is the best known representative, which applies itself to the *why* of human behavior, and deals with motivational determinants.

Perhaps the major contribution to group dynamics was made by Kurt Lewin who focused attention on the complex and shifting nature of group life (Lewin, 1947, 1948, 1951). Lewin emphasized that in a group there is an interdependence of individuals who characterize the "dynamical whole," a change in one sub-part influencing change in the state of any sub-part. Under Lewin's leadership experimental studies attempted to delineate the internal structure, processes, phenomena and laws of group life as well as to apply this data to such practical problems as group productivity, leadership, cohesiveness, etc. that occurred in industry, education, correctional work and other fields. The researches and bibliography in group dynamics have been substantial, including among others the work of French (1941, 1944), Festinger (1942, 1947), Bavelas (1948, 1951), Deutsch (1949, 1951), Cartright (1950), Homans (1950), Bales (1947, 1958), Lippitt (1948) and Hare (1962). The principal experimental work in group dynamics, as will be noted, has been done by social psychologists, although some sociologists have participated, and a psychiatrist, Moreno (1941, 1953), is responsible for "sociometry," the basic model for the study of interpersonal choices. The investigations of greatest interest to the psychotherapist are those that detail the phenomenology of the group rather than those that attempt to explain why the group members behave the way they do, since the instruments employed (attitude scales, etc.) are not considered adequate to reveal motivation in depth.

The concern of psychotherapists with group dynamics is predicated on the basis that behavioral changes are constantly being consummated through the individual's interactions with family, peer, occupational, religious and other groups of which he is a member. Processes may thus be observed taking place within the individual in his relationship with others in the course of which certain kinds of change come about. A study of the dynamics of change illuminates some of the allied operations in individual and particularly group psychotherapy. Moreover, it helps differentiate the contingencies that precipitate out in all groups irrespective of structure from those that are specifically parcels of the psychotherapeutic experience.

Common to all groups are a number of phenomena: (1) All groups possess some kind of structure; (2) the members assume or are assigned special roles; (3) goals toward which the group strives are implicitly accepted or explicitly defined; (4) a communication network mediates the interactions among members; (5) group norms are applied with varying pressure to each individual (social control); and (6) both cohesive and disorganizing forces are at all times operative.

Dynamic interaction is the essence of group activity. Never static, the group constellations alter themseves as new fusions, enmities and alliances allocate different roles for the members. A status hierarchy soon precipitates out which determines the nature and direction of communication. Interacting patterns are evolved which reflect role expectancies.

Many conceptual schemes have been developed to score human interaction, and dynamic themes have been organized around them. Essentially they delineate cognitive task activities in the form of question posing and problem solving (including information collection and evaluation, and the arriving at decisions) and social—emotional reactions, positive and negative; the frequency and duration of contributions to the group; the nature of the communication process, i.e., the manner, content and conditions under which members communicate, with whom they communicate, and to what effect; the productivity of the group in relation to completion of group tasks; the kinds of task behavior manifested, such as observing, hypothesizing and formulating action; the delineation of tendencies to control or be controlled, described in ways such as "authoritarian," "dominating," "submitting," and "democratic"; and the degree of cohesiveness (positive valance) as opposed to disorganization (negative valance) and the forces responsible for both. Groups have been examined from the standpoint of *process,* the activity that goes on in the group; of *structure,* the relations among the components in the group; and of *change* in the structure over a period of time. Behavior in the group is viewed from the standpoint of *interpersonal activity,* what goes on between the members; *intrapersonal activity,* speculations about feelings; and *performances,* what a member does by himself or in a group. Expectations for the roles associated with different positions in the group have been investigated, as have the shared goals, and the delimiting of relationships around sets of norms.

Observation of different groups in operation discloses a number of consistent processes: (1) The individual upon entering a new group brings into it all of the distortions and expectencies which toward him by the other members similarly reflect personal are aspects of his personality structure; while attitudes directed prejudices. These immediate impressions are rectified as interaction continues, perceptions tending to become more reality oriented.

(2) A status struggle often occurs at the beginning of group formation with the establishing of leader-follower hierarchies. Members reach out for leadership on the basis of a number of inner needs, such as identification and dependency. Leadership characteristics are not the same for all groups; they depend on the culture and needs of the group. Intelligence, dominance, self-confidence, vitality, the ability to relate to the goals of the group, and the capacity to participate socially have been found important in all groups.

(3) The norms developed by the group represent rules of behavior designed by the group to achieve its expressed or implied goals. Group norms applied to an individual define his role expectations. The individual also possesses norms that are related to his personal values and goals which may or may not conflict with group norms.

(4) All groups approach one or more of four goals: (a) the group goal of problem solving in relation to some area of concern involving all members (as in a parent-teacher or industrial group); (b) the group goal of resolving expressed or undefined social-emotional problems; for example, shared anxieties (as in an executive training group where group dynamics are emphasized); (c) the goal of supplying an individual in the group with a solution to a personal need (as in a social or educational group); (d) the goal of solving an emotional problem associated with personal and relationship difficulties (as in a therapeutic group).

(5) The structure of the group, and the activities which it sponsors, will, more or less, be modeled by the goals toward which the group directs itself. Generally goals relate to resolution of an explicitly defined external problem that involves the group, or to

a less well defined social-emotional problem within the group which is reflected in shared anxieties.

(6) Group size influences the responses and movement of the group. As numbers in the group increase, information and suggestion giving become more pronounced. This is accompanied by a diminished request for and expression of opinions, and by a lessened agreement among members. Groups of two (dyad) show high tension, avoid antagonism and disputation, ask for opinions, but shy away from giving opinions, and focus on the exchange of information and on reconciliation. In husband-wife pairs, the dominant spouse asks more questions, and expresses more opinions with responses of agreement, disagreement and antagonism. The optimal size of a group is five, a smaller or greater number being less satisfactory to members. Discontentment is expressed if the group gets too large. Each additional member expands the potential relationships among the individuals and subgroups. As the group increases in size, members feel inhibited and threatened, and the leader becomes more removed from the members. Greater difficulty exists in reaching a concensus.

(7) The superiority of group over individual performance has been tested. It has been found that manual productivity is greatest in groups, but intellectual productivity is not necessarily increased. Problem solving within a group framework is enhanced in some individuals, but retarded in others. However group discussion makes individual judgment more accurate. Recall of information is expanded in a group setting.

(8) A variety of situations make for greater group productivity. Productive groups are composed of members whose skills are appropriate for the tasks. The most resourceful and accomplished groups are small, cohesive, of the same sex, have a satisfactory communication network and feedback, and are led by a skillful leader. Autocratic leadership encourages greater quantitative productivity, while democratic leadership results in optimum morale. In authoritarian settings, authoritarian groups achieve greater output; in democratic settings, equalitarian groups are more efficient. Personality characteristics that result in compatibility of individuals in a group and in free communication make for expanded group productivity. Tasks are best accomplished by a group in which rules are appropriate for the tasks.

Where cooperation is expected, there is greater individual incentive, friendliness, communication and productivity; self-oriented needs in a member here tend to disrupt the group. Application of stress, if not too strong, encourages greater productivity; if too strong, the group yield diminishes. Productivity is retarded by any conflicts that develop in the group.

(9) Conflict often appears when the roles of two members clash ("role collision"), where an individual plays two opposing roles ("role incompatibility") and where group members cannot agree as to expected roles ("role confusion"). It also develops where the personality structure of an individual does not coordinate with the role expectation that is dictated by his position in the group. Ethnic, status, intellectual and educational differences among the group members may act as sources of tension and conflict.

(10) Cohesiveness is expanded and disruptive forces are minimized where the members know and like each other, where the prestige of the group is stressed, where members are rewarded on a cooperative rather than competitive basis, where they possess strong mutual interests and are democratically led, and where communication processes are facilitated.

(11) Both deviance and conformity are present in members of a group. The more highly the individual regards the group, the more he needs its prestige, its output, or the friendship of its members, the more he will want to conform. Interactive processes in the group are released by a deviant. This has an effect on group morale, group decisions and cohesiveness. Every group exerts pressures on its members to conform to accepted norms. Where a member deviates in his behavior from the norm, he is subject to one of four choices: he must conform with group norms, he must change his own norms to allign them with those of the group, he must operate as a deviant, or he must retire from the group. Deviant members are pressured to yield to majority opinion, which some will accept. Conformity is encouraged where the majority maintaining a contrary view is large, where membership in the group is valued and where one's opinion must be stated publicly. Yet a minority viewpoint is possible where the minority possess high status, are considered expert or are especially popular. Thus a leader may promote his ideas with the group and find them

accepted even though they clash with sentiments of the group majority; yet the leader will also have to abide by group norms once they are solidified.

Therapeutic Implications

As a consequence of the work of social and role theorists, constructive efforts have been made to study all aspects of group life including the family, the social group, the social institutions, community, race and ethnic relations, social stratification, social mobility and forms of social control that have growth as well as therapeutic potentials. Investigations of the way in which human nature is influenced by group life has brought into the sociological field models derived from psychology with its emphasis upon the individual and the employment of experimental methods. Under the rubric of "social psychology" a number of problems are embraced for study including personality formation, interpersonal relations, mass behavior, social movements, social attitudes, public opinion, propaganda and communication. Particularly relevant to psychotherapists is the study of social change and social disorganization as they interfere with group process and cause deviant behavior in the individual. Political, cultural, economic, technological, demographic and other aspects of social change are related to individual, family and community disorganization which sponsor mental disorder, crime, delinquency, vice, suicide, alcoholism, family tensions, separation, divorce, political corruption, mass unrest, mob behavior and breakdown of social controls.

Since psychotherapy in large measure is concerned with opinion, attitude and value change, the studies conducted by sociologists and social psychologists on the best modes of effectuating such change are important for psychotherapeutic theory and process (Mead, 1934; Lewin, 1935; Bales, 1950).

Following the leads introduced by G. H. Mead (1922) regarding how the child perceives himself as an object when he plays a social role, investigators have explored the influence on individuals of the roles they play in a group, as well as the effect on them of group norms. It has been demonstrated that people can, when working in a group, or when they are convinced they are working in a group, accomplish more in many tasks than when working alone. Membership in a group influences the way the individual perceives reality, his decision making and the nature of his values and prejudices. Often the individual will suppress a correct perception or judgment in favor of the majority opinion, particularly from respected sources, firmly convinced that his conclusions have been independently reached. Where a person is highly motivated to remain in a group, he is more prone to resist arguments, however logical they may be, that are opposed to the group norms. This principle has been found empirically useful in group therapy and group processes, and probably accounts for the dramatic changes that come about in therapeutic and certain social groups (Alcoholics Anonymous, Synanon, etc.) that are hardly possible in individual therapy.

Psychotherapy and group dynamics share in common a goal of altering norms in the individual. The manner in which this change is implemented differs in the two disciplines. Psychotherapy approaches the problem of change by dealing directly with the forces of emotional motivation and conflict; group dynamics operates more peripherally through the influences of group interaction and pressure. Each of the disciplines complements the other. During individual psychotherapy, the patient continues to be permeated by pressures from family, peer and secondary groups. In group psychotherapy, he is in addition subjected to vectors in his therapeutic group.

The pressures of the group for individual conformity are great. A problem posed here is that if group standards are abnormal, it will be difficult for an individual to change a pattern supported or sponsored by his group. Should he alter his behavior in isolation, his deviancy will come under attack when he returns to the group, and he may be forced to assume his previous state. Thus it would seem, as Lewin pointed out, a group change may have to precede transformation in attitudes in a group rooted individual. He may, however, retain his gains if he leaves his customary group for one whose norms are more consonant with his newly developed ones. Or he may assume a leadership role and change the norms of his habitual group to coordinate with his own.

The role a therapist plays with his patients in individual and group therapy is vital. On one end of the scale he may be so authoritarian that he crushes independent strivings in individual therapy and interaction in group therapy; on the other, he may be so passive that he is unable to give the patient essential support or deal with resistance (Durkin, 1964). The work of group dynamic theorists has a bearing on the idea role of the therapist as a leader particularly in a therapy group. Bales (1950) for instance, considers that a leader is one who identifies with the group, has access to resources necessary to achieve the group goal and exerts constantly a constructive influence on the group members. A good group therapist possesses all of these qualities. The question of whether more is accomplished by being participating rather than supervisory is answered in studies which show that opinion change is fostered more by free discussion and feedback than by lectures or directives. It is particularly important that the leader avoid strong authoritarianism (Preston and Heintz, 1949). This does not mean that strong leadership is destructive; it may be constructive where the leader permits others to participate and take the initiative if they wish (Bonner, 1959). Cooperative groups are more productive and achieve a common goal more easily than competitive groups (Deutsch, 1949). Individuals in a group who operate with self-oriented needs rather than for group needs hamper the group movement (Fourezios et al., 1950).

In molding opinion change it has been discovered that in issues difficult for the subject to understand, he is swayed most by persuasive arguments of an "expert," while in more familiar issues his opinions are prone to greatest change when he comes to his own conclusions. Appeals to action based on fear will, if too tension producing, tend to be disregarded, possibly as an effort to repress anxiety. On the other hand, fears that are less frightening will motivate the subject to act. Persuasion is most effective where the individual attends to an argument, comprehends it and, inspired by a need within himself, assimilates it. Researches indicate that if a person whose attitudes one seeks to change can be convinced to play the role of an experimenter persuading others to alter their opinions, he will eventually come under the influence of his own arguments. Some of these findings may be incorporated in psychotherapeutic interviewing techniques; for instance, by (1) making the therapist's communications clear to the patient, (2) providing him with proper information and cues in order that he may come to insights and decisions on his own, (3) reducing his anxiety sufficiently before making any appeals for action, and (4) encouraging psychodramatic role playing, the patient acting the part of persuader in changing the opinions of a subject in the direction the patient himself must move.

Festinger (1957) has presented a theory to the effect that attitude change is fostered by a need to resolve discrepancies in perception (cognitive dissonance). Thus if a person with Victorian sexual values comes under the influence of a respected authority who advocates freedom of sexual expression, he will, to restore balance in his cognitive field, either have to become less sexually repressed or lose his respect for the authority. A maintenance of a positive working relationship with the patient is thus crucial in bringing about any kind of value change. Since group acceptance, an important human need, is contingent on realizing and pursuing the norms of the group (Homans, 1950), a good therapeutic group, the values of whose members are not too deviant from the norm, is a helpful tool toward change. Mutual interaction in the group must, however, be fostered.

The effects of social, role and group dynamic theory on the field of psychotherapy have been vast influencing ego-analytic and neo-freudian movements, as well as such therapeutic systems as psychodrama, sociodrama, transactional therapy, group therapy, family therapy and social therapy. The force of environmental factors in initiating and sustaining emotional illness has also focused attention on casework and environmental manipulation as important adjuncts in psychotherapy.

X

Cultural Anthropology

WHILE BIOLOGY GIVES BASIC NEEDS THEIR BODY, CULTURE SHAPES their form and mode of expression. Moreover, superimposed on biologic needs are many drives nurtured by the culture or subculture within the individual's society that become motivational sources in their own right. The reciprocal relationship that exists between personality and culture has focused interest on the part of psychotherapists on the methods and findings of cultural anthropology.

At about the time Freud began his work, anthropology also came into being. For many years anthropologists worked in preliterate societies. The question continually arose as to whether or not the observations and inferences gleaned from their work could be employed as a model for the understanding of the behavior of what was termed the "civilized people." Freud was very much aware of the atavistic impulses in civilized persons, but he was not too sensitive to his cultural biases and to the fact that the behavior of his sex repressed Viennese patients was greatly influenced by the cultural patterning governing sex in the Victorian age. In the last twenty-five years, anthropologists have studied a great variety of cultural groups including the more "sophisticated" ones of Europe and the United States, and have not limited themselves to the pre-literate. On the basis of these investigations, anthropologists have pointed out that the latter, the pre-literate, also have a long cultural history that has evolved into quite elaborate rituals and modes of behavior, a study of which may help us understand better our own cultural patternings (Roheim, 1950; Kardiner, 1939, 1945).

Anthropology in its broadest sense deals with the fields of archaeology, physical anthropology, linguistics and ethnology, or cultural or social anthropology. By studying the evidences of man's existence prior to his written recordings through excavating the remains of ancient human activity (dwellings, tombs, implements, weapons, art, settlement patterns, etc.), archaeologists provide information on material culture and their possible effect on the inner life of the involved people (Boas, 1938). Linguistics, probing as it does into vital aspects of communication, yields clues regarding the culture of a group and the means it employs for the organization of reality. It is also a vehicle for the understanding of cognitive processes, personality and the structure of human behavior (Hymes, 1962). Ethnology, which focuses on the origin, history, customs and institutions of the different population groups, has provided an understanding of homologous behavioral patterns common to all mankind, as well as unique patterns distinctive for a culture. Cultural anthropologists, interested in the interrelationship of culture and personality, examine features of societies that sponsor unique patterns, and they try to identify the forces in the environment that influence the development of universal as well as singular institutions and personality traits.

The methods of anthropology are basically comparative. Hypotheses and theories about a given society are tested empirically in other societies, which may possess different historical traditions. In this way, rules for behavior and institutionalized behavior of individuals are subjected to scrutiny. Additionally, cross cultural comparisons are made of social institutions dealing with economic, political, social, organizational, religious, artistic, health and other practices, as well as world view and value systems. Correlations are attempted to determine their relationship to specific types of individual character structure, as well as to constructive or destructive influences on society as a whole. The importance of this type of information is becoming more apparent with expanding international exchange of research data. For example, studies of delinquency, suicide, drug addiction, alcoholism and other social maladies indicate some common etiological factors in all societies which provide leads toward prevention. Working with living people in contemporary societies, anthropologists are frequently involved in multidisciplinary research.

A sub-field called by some "psychological anthropology" (Hsu, 1961) attempts to apply dynamic concepts to anthropological material. For example, interesting psychoanalytic interpretations of ethnological data presented to him by anthropologists have been made by Kardiner (1939; 1945), which detail the basic kinds of personality structure that evolve from child rearing practices, through values imposed on the individual in the educational process, and through the institutional modes offered him for the expression, denial, repression and sublimination of his basic needs, particularly, aggression and sexuality. Generally espoused is the contention that Freud's notion of culture as a product of the biological needs of mankind (La Barre, 1958) and of social institutions as mere precipitates of innate sexual and aggressive drives are inadequate conceptualizations of a phenomenon possessing many complex vectors that require consideration of cognitive processes and ego psychology.

In exploring such vectors, cultural anthropologists have related themselves to and have been influenced by a number of disciplines including psychiatry, genetics, ethnology, physiology, sociology and psychology (Mead, 1963; Wallace, 1961, 1962; Arieti, 1956; Ruesch, 1959; Spiegel, 1959; Sapir, 1937; Linton, 1956; Hutchinson, 1965). Out of this alliance a number of interesting and important contributions have materialized, as in relation to the effect of selected cultures on personality growth, the impact of cultural institutions on emotional conflict, the consequences of cultural change and culture conflict, the epidemiology of psychiatric symptoms and syndromes, and the stressful effects of role and value incompatibility in different cultures (Spiro, 1958; Du Bois, 1963; Lewis, 1963; Padilla, 1958; Keesing, 1959; Wallace, 1961; Opler, 1958, 1959, 1965; Srole, 1962; Leighton, 1959). Recognizing the importance of early experience for full maturation of the adult sexual and parental roles, such as has been demonstrated by Harlow (1961) in rhesus monkeys, some of the observations have focused on neonate mother and peer interactions in the different societies (Whiting, 1963).

Among the generalizations pertinent to personality theory that have emerged from cross cultural studies are the following: (1) People brought up in the same society are subjected to many similar influences and, as a consequence, manifest certain common behavioral characteristics. The language they speak, the customs they observe, the general world view they envisage are more prone to be alike than those of citizens of different societies. Individual variations nevertheless will exist because of differing genetic and experiential determinants. (2) The adjusted individual in any society espouses, more or less, the value systems of that society. (3) Character structure reflects the value systems of the culture. Where values oppose the constructive expression of basic needs, and adequate institutional expression in substitutive form is not provided, the character structure will manifest certain distortions. (4) Parental deviations from standard cultural values will tend to influence deviations in the offspring from the characterologic norm of the society. (5) Although there may be striking similarities in physical and emotional growth among all societies, there are wide differences due to a variety of factors. For instance, physical growth varies because of nutritional and disease influences. Emotional differences can be very extensive also due to different cultural patterns. Thus some societies repress sex and allow free aggression; others do the exact opposite. (6) The patterns and styles of expressing the shared needs and drives of mankind are widely diversified and make for a heterogeneity of traits that distinguish one cultural group from another. (7) Cultural aspects of behavior are of "learned" or "acquired" origin, not of genetic origin. (8) It is vital to recognize that "average" is a matter of definition and that the distinction between "average" and "deviation from average" reflects cultural discriminations.

Some studies of mental and emotional syndromes in countries where ethnic and class identifications are well defined have attempted to delineate the similarities and divergencies in symptom manifestations and to relate them to variations in the culture (Tooth, 1950; Opler, 1958, 1959, 1965; Srole, 1962). "Cultural psychiatry," drawing from many of the findings of cultural anthropology, considers basic personality stress influences that are present in a culture and the effect of cultural institutions on the forms of illness and modes of coping with these (Wittkower and Rin, 1965). While schizophrenia and manic-depressive psychosis may easily be identified, other syndromes are cloaked in different symbolic raiment. Symptomatic manifestations in all syndromes are influenced by the culture. For example, special hysterical and psychosomatic phenomena are endemic in certain societies. Thus the Eskimo "pibloktog," the Northeastern American Indian "windigo," the Southeast Asian "amok," "koro" and "latah" phenomena, the Japanese "kitsunetsuki," and the South American "susto" are unique in their external forms, though the underlying conflicts are not dissimilar to those seen in Western cultures. Interesting cross cultural studies on trance and possession have been made which show the affiliation of Afro-Brazilian (Hutchinson, 1957), African, Caribbean, South American and other trance and toxic states, induced by religious ceremonies or ritual drugs, with Western trance manifestations during religious revival meetings, and with the toxic effects in Western peoples of mescaline, LSD and other psychotomimetic drugs. Schizophrenic delusions and hallucinations depend for their content on the prevailing magical animistic bias, while the form of schizophrenia (excitements, catatonia, etc.) relate often to cultural factors which put a premium on certains forms of behavior. Alcoholism, drug addiction, delinquency, psychopathic personality, depression, obsessional neurosis and other disorders are proportionately greater in some societies than in others, constituting, where prevalent, more commonly accepted means of impulse fulfillment as well as defense. Psychoneurotic problems are rampant among all cultures, primitive or advanced, but the types may vary. Thus acute anxiety reactions of short duration and hysterical reactions are more common in primitive societies, while obsessional neuroses are less common than in civilized societies. A hypothesis that emerges from studies of shifting symptom pictures within a society, is that changing social conditions result in altered psychopathology. Within a society difference in the prevalence of certain syndromes may be observed. For example, hysterical manifestations appear more frequently among uneducated rural populations than in urban communities. Tolerance of neurotic and psychotic individuals in the community will depend on how close their symptoms approximate the accepted norm. In some cultures schizophrenic detachment, mysticism and reality distortion are regarded as God-given, the victim being easily absorbed as a respected member or official in a religious order. In other cultures, he may become classified as an outcast. Unfortunately cross cultural studies of emotional problems bring up our contemporary limitations in diagnostic criteria which will hopefully be rectified with continuing research and the exchange of information on an international level.

By application of the methods of participant observation developed originally in the field study of nonliterate small societies, anthropologists have studied the social interaction in and culture of psychiatric hospitals and wards, and have investigated manners in which societies in different parts of the world cope with the mentally ill. Studies on the speech patterns (pitch, intonations, sound formation) of schizophrenics through the use of anthropological linguistics have also been an area of inquiry by some anthropologists, such as Birdwhistle.

Anthropology is among the social sciences involved in the presently expanding field of community mental health and social psychiatry, and it has contributed with medicine, social psychology, sociology, and public health toward the promotion of a better adjustment in family, interpersonal, occupational, educational, social, religious and recreational pursuits. The special problems occurring in rural, suburban and urban areas and their effect on the incidence and character of emotional illness have been subjected to interdisciplinary study (Opler, 1958, 1965; Mead, 1963; Leighton, 1959, 1960, 1963; Srole, 1962).

The susceptibility of different cultural groups to our present-day approaches in mental health is of concern to the psychotherapist. Since cultural symbols and values are the medium through which the individual patient approaches what is offered him in psychotherapy, his responses to the stratagems of the therapist will be circumscribed by the meaning they have for him in terms of his general life view (Devereux, 1953; Burgum, 1957; Abel, 1956, 1965). Thus offering a neurotic individual sophisticated insights, born of the principles of psychic determinism, will prove futile if his cultural orientation convinces him that he is being invaded by evil spirits. Suggestion and legerdemain will have a greater effect. Prevalent cultural values and social philosophies will also support and suppress certain therapeutic trends. Accordingly while the Soviet countries gear themselves to Pavlovian approaches minimizing psychoanalytic viewpoints, Western countries sponsor dynamic insight as the important tactic, while Asian countries are more attuned to philosophic ideas. With increased communication among scientists, that brings conceptual frames of reference into common perspective, a blending of credos and doctrines is to be expected.

Finally the field research activities of anthropologists have provided some important leads on how to prepare populations for rapid changes in social organization, such as are occurring today in underdeveloped countries, urban renewal areas, suburban monoclass communities, civil rights movements, etc., which necessitate new roles and open up educational opportunities that conflict with traditional positions and values. These clues are potentially valuable in helping to deal with reactions toward the contempory shifts from feudalism to democracy, from agrarianism to industrialism, from colonialism to independence which so often tax coping capacities. They are important too in handling the adjustment problems wrought by massive migration from rural to urban communities, by influx of foreign groups into a new society, and by the breakdown of class and racial barriers which necessitate a living together of peoples who habitually have distrusted one another.

XI

Communication Theory; Information Theory; Cybernetics

Twentieth century technology is characterized by start-ling advances in the science of communication. To accommodate the complex instrumentation developed for the transmission and processing of information, attempts have been made to develop a unifying theory which in essence reduces to mathematical terms the operative principles of systems that discharge and manipulate information. In recent years theories and concepts from the area of communication have been increasingly applied to the psycho-logical field, the language of communication being employed to delineate intrapsychic and interpersonal operations.

Technology is the child of mechanics which originally dealt solely with the transmission of force and the storing of energy in the form of mechanical strain. With the development of the heat machine during the Industrial Revolution, machines assumed the function not only of storing, but of transforming energy. Prin-ciples of thermodynamics were accordingly applied to technolog-ical activities. A further evolution took place with the develop-ment of machines with control centers which were able to transfer information to its constituent internal parts as well as to other machines. Out of these discoveries there have emerged a group of postulates pertaining to machine behavior some aspects of which appear to apply to human behavior.

Communications Theory

Communications theory is actually not a theory, but a tech-nology that, embodying physical, psychological and sociological aspects of communication, attempts to establish parallels in the communication of information among machines, organ systems and institutions. The communications unit common to all of these entities consists essentially of a "source" which sends information via a "transmitter" to a "destination," which admits the information through a "receiver." The source selects the "message," "encodes" it into transmissible "signals," and transmits it as "output" to the "input" of a destination where it is "decoded." In human communication the system that emits signals (the source) is a person who influences a receiving system in the form of another person. The message to be relayed through the "communication channel," symbolically processed by the brain, is encoded into signals and transmitted by the muscles that emit sounds, words and gestures. This "output" acts as an "input" stimulus impinging on the sense organs of the receiving agency. Neural impulses are transmitted to the brain and the signals are decoded into meaningful messages that deal with significant aspects of the perceived stimulus. The individual, according to communication theory, acts as a channel, i.e., as a system that transmits a signal from an input location (sense organ) to an output location (motor mechanism). The study of the apparatus of communication systems, including the human system, is in terms of physics and engineering.

Choices of messages transmitted involve certain probabilities. Thus, if there are N equally likely possibilities in the selection of messages, the measure of information may be scored as $\log_2 N$. Because the formula for the amount of possible information is identical with equations representing entropy in statistical mechanics, a relationship to thermodynamics is presumed. Measures for encoding information and for establishing the capacity of a channel have been estimated. Experimental work on band limited channels, filtering and prediction has also been extensive and the findings are being applied to the fields of cryptology, linguistics and psychology. Relationships have been shown to exist between the quantity of information contained in a stimulus and the reaction time to the stimulus. It is firmly assumed that failure in communication is responsible for problems in symbolic functioning, and for defects in essential semantic operations that relate to the establishing of meaning. Communication difficulties are also believed to be at the basis of problems in social interaction in group situations. In summary, it is speculated that man in manipulating information adopts codes and methods similar to those employed in communication theory.

Information Theory

The process of sending information in telecommunication involves an affiliated body of knowledge, often referred to as "information theory," which is concerned with the study of the transmission of messages and signals. Here, in addition to physics and engineering, linguistic, psychological and sociological data are utilized toward the understanding of physical representations that have meaning and content. From this, hypotheses have been developed about nervous functioning and behavior. For example, the coding operations of amplitude and freqency modulation in telecommunication seem also to exist in the synaptic transmission of signals within the nervous system (MacKay and McCulloch, 1952). By studying electrical switching operations, ideas have emerged concerning the functional interaction of neurons (Shannon, 1938). The solving of logical problems by computing machines which are programmed to execute specific tasks have led to theories about how memory, associations and thinking relate to the organization of networks of relays (theories of automata). Human problem solving and other aspects of neocortical functioning, which depend on a hierarchial ordering of the central nervous system, may, it is believed, be approached through information input from the environment. In one second as many as one million to one hundred million signals enter the neocortex through the perceptual apparatus. The neocortex fixes perception of reality, selecting aspects that are important to its needs, subjecting these to ordered processing and categorization, and yet remaining flexibly open to new information to correct deficiencies. Illustrative of defective information handling is schizophrenia, in which an inability to select appropriate information results in the excluding of relevant items and the inclusion of irrelevant data in relation to categorization (Rothstein, 1965).

Cybernetics

In recent years a movement has developed among some scientists to examine social phenomena through the structure of the nervous system of interacting organisms. Students of mathematical biology, like Nicolas Rashevsky, have attempted to explain human behavior by physico-mathematical references. For instance, they have developed a neurophysiological model for the study of the individual and society. Hypotheses of how two nerve cells interact have been extended to delineate interactions within widespread neural systems, and to account for individual and group behavior and even society itself.

Engineers working on electronic calculating machines and automatic regulatory and control mechanisms have also tried to apply their discoveries to the human nervous system. The insights of communications engineering, blended with neurophysiology and information theory, and extended to neural, psychic and social functioning has resulted in a science of "cybernetics." Thus Norbert Wiener employed the mathematical theory of electronic networks to neural networks in individuals. From this he postulated societies as systems of communicative networks. Wiener put stress on "feedback" as a principal device in both machines and man. Thus governing machines function by having information fed back to them which indicates when a system is not performing as intended. The mechanism (servo-mechanism) then sets into motion processes to rectify the error. An example of this is the thermostatic control of a heating plant which, when the temperature is too low, releases devices to manufacture more heat. The heat regulating mechanism of the human body appears to operate similarly. The individual possesses many feedback contrivances to restore the homeostatic balance. Cybernetics contends that even societies depend for their survival on the communicative "feedback" of information that indicates when they are not functioning well and that sets into motion essential reparative processes.

According to cybernetics, man is a subtle machine infinitely more complex than the most elaborate electronic computer, but subject to the same laws of learning and communication. The human machine encompasses a bewildering number of operations. The brain alone contains ten billion neurons, the patterns of whose interaction are so elaborate that the number of potential connections have been calculated at $_2(10,000,000,000)^2$, which is a greater number than the aggregate of every electron, proton and neutron in the universe. Cybernetics presumes to have developed a means of scientific approach to the complexities of the human system.

These assumptions are obviously speculative, but rich hypotheses have emerged from them, for instance, those that deal with the principles of homeostasis and permit interesting experiments into some of the part functions of mental activity. The transfer activities of servo-mechanisms enable neurophysiologists to speculate about the properties of brain structures and to map their functions (Rapoport, 1959). A study of the breakdown of servo-mechanisms suggested to Wiener (1948) that nervous pathology followed some of the same laws, a hunch that has been corroborated.

The concept of feedback systems conceives of the brain as dynamically involved in coding, analyzing, remembering and interpreting messages, constantly working, processing perceptual input, organizing immediate data in relationship to the data of past experience, and fusing functions with creative planning for the fufillment of various needs. It is not too bizarre to assume that we may someday be able to explain many psychological maneuvers in purely physical terms. Important leads toward this end have emerged from the field of cybernetics.

Summary. According to communication and information theorists, the thinking function may be conceived of as a processing system in which stored combinations of symbolic information program definite behavior sequences (Simon, 1964). As such the study of machines that receive, process, store and release information may yield clues about the workings of the human brain. In interpreting brain function, cybernetic concepts of system instability and feedback mechanisms have been employed (Harvey, 1965 a, b). Moreover mathematical theorums applicable to control devices have been applied to the regulatory and control mechanisms of the brain. Some observers have even assumed the existence of a "deviation-amplifying" mutual causal action in both machines and the brain in which a small disruption of homeostasis is amplified by positive feedback and then leads to more pronounced effects than could be explained by the minor intensity of the initial stimulus (Maruyama, 1963).

Though some reasonable assumptions may be made from the study of mechanical systems, conclusions are at best tentative and apply only to a few of the existent operations. For instance, the reverberating circuit notion of memory storage, employed in digital computers applies to only one kind of crude storage activity that may go on in the brain. Much more sophisticated mechanisms must exist considering the vast amount of material stored in the relatively compact space of the neuron, which involve memory-encoded units of DNA. It is naive to assume that any man-made machine can provide complete answers to the storage pursuits of the brain since every molecule of DNA contains a greater potential storehouse of information than the potential capacity of the largest computer (Bell, 1962).

Manifestly, the material from communications theory, information theory and cybernetics cannot at this time account for all of the complexities of human activity. Attempts to explain behavior by referring to the science of physical systems are only partially successful, since physical systems deal with a relatively small number of parameters and behavior is infinitely reticular. Ideas like "homeostasis," "feedback" and "thermodynamics" are interesting, but this does not justify their extension into the world of ideation. The transfer of the language of the physical sciences to behavioral functions ("input," "information," "overload," etc.) is particularly irrelevant and confusing. However, aspects of the physical and mechanical operations of communication, and of control, regulatory and feedback forces in the organism have been clarified through the use of these theories. Extrapolations from the operations of the physical systems are useful only as avenues toward hypothetical formulation. Serious problems arise where global assumptions are adduced from these theories toward generalizations that cover the entirety of intrapsychic, interpersonal and social phenomena.

XII

Philosophy, Religion and the Problem of Values

RESIDUES OF ONTOLOGICAL DEVELOPMENT, ACCRETIONS OF CUL-
ture, and other patternings of learning are registered indelibly in
the individual in the form of values and meaning systems that sit
astride the mind and power a great many of its operations. In the
hierarchy of mental functioning these systems occupy the highest
post. Psychotherapy deals with the discovery and understanding
of those values that interfere with a proper adjustment, and it
strives to help the individual to acquire new constructive modes
of thinking, feeling and behaving. Philosophy, whose premises are
verifiability and interpretation, approaches through inductive inference the substance of value and meaning. Religion proposes
ways of shaping values toward loftier moral goals, such as the
unselfish concern for one's fellow men.

The predicaments of the human being living in a finite world
with pervasive stress and conflict, confused about his identity,
facing dehumanizing experiences, and confronted with the inevitability of death, have forced him to evolve philosophies that
cushion his emotions, and to turn to powers higher than himself
for solace and security. Because people in one way or another
evolve inner philosophical systems that justify and rationalize their
life motifs, and because they reach toward religion to supply them
with formulas for achieving inner peace and freedom from fear,
psychotherapists are interested in the purpose and consequence of
such maneuverings. Indeed, some psychotherapists, convinced that
both philosophy and religion are fruitful adjunctive instrumentalities that can help their patients adapt themselves more pur-
posefully to life, incorporate philosophic and religious principles
into their therapeutic schemes.

In considering the virtues or liabilities of such an amalgamation, questions such as the following pose themselves: (1) What aspects of mental functioning may best be approached through the avenues of philosophic or religious experience? (2) In what ways do philosophy and religion alleviate emotional stress and support a productive adjustment? (3) Are neurotic constituents kept alive or exaggerated by the adoption of certain philosophic systems or the pursuit of special religious practices? (4) Can philosophical and religious ideas serve as sources of conflict, and if so under what circumstances?

Ultimately, successful psychotherapy must accomplish an alteration in the patient's sense of values. These, accretions of many units, fashion drives and action tendencies that operate in the service of adaptation. Many of the value systems are products of the individual's cultural heritage, subtly passed along through educational promptings. These embody moral codes whose origins date back to the earliest phases of man's history, the lineage of social tradition, redesigned to conform with the sanctions of the modern world. Many are the protocols of parental prescripts, incorporating neurotic ideologies; or the product of pleasureable biological drives or their sublimated derivatives; or the reverberations of self-needs; or responses to anxiety; or credendas of the conscience that deal with issues of duty, responsibility, obligation to others and to the world. The sum total of these values, alternating, fluctuating, fusing, receding, makes for the uniqueness of the individual, more or less determining the quality of his adaptations. A consideration of values is, for the psychotherapist, of fundamental importance, not only in terms of detecting sources of conflict, but also of working toward goals in therapy, in service of the end results he ideally seeks to achieve. A review of the evolvement of values may be of more than didactic interest.

The importance of a historical perspective on philosophic and religious values lies in the fact that our contemporary western culture embodies a profusion of Socratic, Epicurian, Platonic, Aristotelian, Stoical, Sceptical, Jewish and Christian ideologies which subtly influence the values of modern man in support of or in contradiction to his basic biological and humanistic needs, the economic and political forces operating on and around him, and the scientific and technological developments which have restructured his physical universe. Many conflicts, the result of value discordances, are traditionally accepted as aspects of man's nature without challenging their origins. Such value conflicts may be seen in patients struggling to liberate themselves from neurotic difficulties. They may be observed in psychotherapists themselves, who, in their efforts to teach their patients new values, may perpetuate their personal maladaptive ones which they often tag as standard.

Ancient philosophic interests. Philosophy, a Greek word, whose meaning embraces the love or pursuit of wisdom and of "mental excellence," is concerned with the dialectical or analytical inquiry about meaning, as distinguished from science which relates itself to the empirical inquiry about fact. Essentially, it devotes itself to a dialectical clarification of concepts. Among its divisions are *epistemology,* the theory of knowledge as reflected in language, belief and experience; *metaphysics,* which embraces ideas of substance, causality and the relations of the sciences; *aesthetics,* the rational and a priori aspects of the beautiful; *logic,* the systematic study of valid inference; and *ethics,* the scrutiny of moral judgements and values. While other aspects of philosophy are of some interest to the psychotherapist, the realm of values is of most penetrating concern.

The earliest philosophers dedicated themselves to speculations regarding the origins and operations of the world as a revolt against concepts that credited cosmologies to the capriciousness of the Gods. The basic substance out of which the world was presumed to be fashioned could not be described, but its nature was believed to be within the range of rational understanding. There was in these pre-Socratic times great speculation about such entities as mass and movement. It was little wonder that the science of mathematics evolved from these creative imaginings, and what we now call science, like biology, astronomy, etc., emerged as a consequence of such explorations. During the era of Socrates and the Sophists, philosophic inquiry shifted toward a moral and practical focus. Logic and the theory of knowledge became popular areas for contemplation.

Around the third century B.C., social conditions sponsored interest in ethics, particularly systems which favored the pursuit of mental tranquility. The values inherent in such systems were not fortuitous, nor were they the felicitous improvisations of genius. They were the outcroppings of many vectors, political, economic, and cultural, that dominated a historical period and found expression in the teachings and writings of scholars and savants who took refuge in certain ideologies as tokens of their idiosyncratic natures or personality distortions. Because they were prepared for them, such formulas found receptive eyes and ears among the populace. A recapitulation of some of the cardinal doctrines is important not only topologically, but also because it chronicles modes of thinking which are still exploited today for the purpose of achieving tranquility.

Knowledge and reason as primary values. Socrates (470-399 B. C.) is generally credited with the sponsorship of the value that knowledge is the measure of the highest human achievement. Leading the stormy life of a rebel, Socrates assumed the mission of imparting to mankind the supreme importance of rational understanding. His legacy to philosophy was the contention that reason had a practical purpose in formulating a rule of life. This rule for Socrates was the search for knowledge of the absolutely "good" as the prime condition for well-being. Plato (428-348 B. C.), a contemporary and disciple of Socrates, accenting Socrates' contention that "virtue is knowledge," contended that only reason could subordinate man's "spirit" and "body desires" to courage and temperence. However, few select people, favored by birth, talent, wealth and education, could control reasonably their lower nature and deal with life with justice and wisdom. The rest of the populace were relegated to living on a practical level being governed by belief and opinion. Aristotle (384-322 B. C.), too, extolled the contemplation of knowledge as the essence of life insisting that moral principles had to be discovered inductively. Socratic, Platonic and Aristotelian sponsorship of a rational, moral personality capable of insight into the true scale of "good" for many years dominated the ethical scene.

Values of pleasure and freedom from pain. In a different direction was subordination of reason to the principle of pleasure. This was the value sponsored by Aristippus (435-356 B. C.), the spokesman of the Cyrenaics, who proposed sentient pleasure for the moment as the highest good irrespective of the consequences. This Hedonistic principle was subjected to many interpretations. Theodorus, for instance, proposed that the avoidance of pain and things painful was a greater expediency than sheer dedication to the search for pleasure. Thus mental pain was to be eliminated by regarding with indifference such propositions as poverty and riches, slavery and freedom, death and life. Parading prudence as the guardian of pleasure, Epicurus (341-270 B. C.) proclaimed "pleasure to be the beginning and end of a blessed life; for we recognize this to be our first and natural good, and from this we start in every choice and avoidance; and this we make our goal, using feeling as the canon by which we judge every good." Since many pleasures entailed more than their worth in future pain, pleasures were to be carefully selected for "it is not possible to live pleasantly without living wisely and well and righteously." Happiness was residual in quiet of mind, hence the two great fears in life—fear of the gods and fear of death—were to be eliminated as much as possible from man's thinking.

Self-mastery and moral duty.   Reaction against the Hedonists and Epicurians was to be expected on the part of those who could not countenance the indulgence of pleasure in any form. This protest found expression in the philosophies of the Cynics and Stoics. Antisthenes (365 B. C.) and Diogenes (fl. 4th century B. C.) are credited with sponsorship of the Cynical principle of studied disregard of pleasure, which like other aspects of human desire were to be considered evil. Perfect well-being could be achieved only by self-mastery, detachment and independence from the promptings of pleasure. Poverty, disrepute, and severe toil were useful in achieving spiritual freedom and virtue. Zeno (320-250 B. C.), founder of the Stoical movement, preached strict conformity to the divine will. The pursuit of practical goodness and the learning of virtue by exercise, effort and training were staunchly espoused, tinctured with a religious dogma that lent sanction to moral duty. Desire and passion were contaminants of the soul to be dealt with by indifference. Pleasure and pain, inescapable ingredients of life, were to be borne with a calm that revealed neither joy nor grief. Only through moral responsibility could man avoid error. To live by wisdom was the supreme good, the avenue to peace of mind.

Scepticism. Concurrent with other ancient systems, and emerging as a revolt against dogmatic, entrenched and effete points of view, was the evolvement of the philosophy of doubting. Scepticism firmly denied the possibility of knowing reality on the basis that the human mind by its constitution could not ever appreciate the ultimate nature of reality. Thus the Sophists reacted against the Greek cosmologists. Gorgias (483-375 B. C.), in his writings expressed three principles of sceptical nihilism: (1) nothing exists; (2) if it did exist we would not be able to know about it; (3) if we did know about it we could not communicate what we knew. The first well-formulated system that supported scepticism was organized by Pyrrho (360-270 B. C.) approximately three hundred years before Christ. Since, claimed Pyrrho, real knowledge was impossible, attempts to define what was true or untrue could lead only to stress and discomfort. Accordingly, it was wise as the highest value to impugn the senses, to avoid definite conclusions, to withdraw into oneself and to show an imperturbability of emotion or *ataraxia* (from which, incidentally, the term "ataractic" as used for such drugs as Miltown or Librium is derived.)

Neoplatonic mystical values of union with the Absolute. Through the second century A. D. the schools of Plato, Aristotle, Epicurus, Pyrrho and Zeno contended for a supreme position in the ethical thinking of the western world. Plotinus (205-270 A. D.), in a Neoplatonic movement, identified "good" with the pure existence of the soul and its function of reason, which could escape the contagion of the body's animal impulses. Purification of the soul from such contagion constituted the highest virtue, the most intense human experience being constituted by the soul's apprehension of its union with the divine. Such an experience borders on mystic ecstacy. One may see in its mystical components some similarities between Neoplatonism and oriental theosophy. In both there is a thrust toward experience beyond knowledge and a turning away from the body and the world. A kind of salvation and deliverance is achieved by ecstatic union with the One.

Religious values of Faith, Love, Purity and Chastity. From earliest times society has provided in the form of religion a prolific institutional outlet for humanity's spiritual needs. Gods were evolved in the pattern of man's designs, with powers to enrich harvests, to mitigate sufferings, to banish illness and eliminate death. Hallowed temples were built for worship. A priesthood was developed possessed of ritual purity and other properties restricted to the sacred. Prayers were organized through which souls might beseech the divine, and sacrifices were offered as brides. Atonements reestablished spiritual purification. Rules were layed down and firmed up into canons. There were cleansing rituals for stated defilements, and apotropaic rites for the expulsion of evil. Religion gradually assumed a personal flavor as a means of salvation or redemption, and prophetic figures, devoting themselves with burning zeal to its inner forms, diverted religion from its formal institutional base toward personal values. Satisfaction by religion of personal needs introduced in man the desire for an intimate relation with the Almighty to share in his glory, to gain his beneficences, to assuage suffering and deliverance from evil. The craving for unity with one absolute God as an aspect of these needs fashioned the developing monotheism, which, as may have been predicted, contained many relics of pagan lineage. The universal principle of the One identified by the Babylonians as "Marduk," the Greeks as "Moira," the Persians as "Asha," the Egyptians of the Middle Kingdom as "Ra," the Hindus as "Karma" and "Rita," the Chinese as "Tao," at first contained many aspects of pantheism. The initiating of the faithful into the service of God joined believers in their goal toward enrichment of their personal lives toward the organization of Churches dissociated from the secular community. Deliverance from moral evil followed rites of repentence and expressions of faith; redemption promised participation in the divine life. Revelation from divine sources through visions, dreams, omens and personal inspiration and "possession" was one aspect of monotheism. Thus Zarathustra disclosed the holy message from Ahura Mazda eight hundred years before Christ, and Jahveh proclaimed himself to the prophets of Israel as a righteous God who demanded righteousness in his followers. Revelations were recorded in sacred books as manifestations of the divine truth and formed, with a growing body of doctrines, the basis for religion. Embodied were codes of ethics by which the believer was to fashion his behavior. Moral laws become divine commands. Along with this the ultimate destiny of man and of the world was posited. Such eschatological ideas were more or less oriented around the value of the individual in his present society, as well as the fate to which he was to be assigned in terms of rewards and punishments in the future life.

Social conditions supported a spread of a new brand of moral consciousness throughout the Greco-Roman civilization, in the form of a written code, presumably originating in divine revelation, and sanctioned by divine promises of rewards and threats of punishments. Whereas discipline in polytheism was present by implication, the concept of one Almighty God who demanded unquestioned submission, who issued divine commands as contained in official scripture or interpreted by inference, was much more compelling. Jewish theology, from which later Christianity was derived, contemplated moral insight which was sponsored by a divine edict emanating from sources outside of human reason, as interpreted by Moses and the later prophets. Christianity, rejecting the ceremonial part of the Jewish decrees and the existing system of ecclesiastical jurisprudence as dictated by Rabbinic erudition, accepted God's law as contained in the sacred books of the Jews, supplementing it with the teaching of Christ and his apostles.

Permeating the ethics of the new Christian order was the idea of Christian goodness. It was to be expected that relics of pagan ethical philosophy would become a component part of the early Christian philosophy, influencing values regarding the promotion of virtue, suppression of inner vicious desires and rightness of purpose. But ancient knowledge and wisdom, prime forces in the ancient philosophies, were, in the new order, subordinated to the agencies of Faith and Love. Faith in the divine law demanded a subordination of reason to will, the acceptance of Christ as the leader in the battle with evil, and ruler of the kingdom to be realized. Faith endowed the believer, through God's supernatural aid or grace, with a goodness which he could not otherwise attain. Man was a sinner at birth, deserving utter condemnation; but God in his justness could be benevolent toward him because of the perfect services and suffering of Christ. The second central theme in Christianity of Love, springing from Christian Faith was the principle moral value of Christian Duty expressed in devotion to God and to all mankind as objects of God's love and participants in the humanity shared by the incarnation. Christian morality also enshrined Purity which made mandatory the repression of vicious desires under threats of punishment by an avenging divinity. Obedience, benevolence, hope, unworldliness, purity and humility, qualities inherent in the life and precepts of Christ, became the principal Christian virtues.

Christianity as a true code of conduct sanctioned by eternal rewards and punishments was subject to many interpretations in different societies in which it became the chief religion. In essence its ethical view was centered in the moral teaching of Jesus Christ as contained in the Sermon on the Mount and in the apostolic teaching which became the standard for the deciding of moral conduct. By example, by parable, by proposition Jesus propounded certain philosophies as the basis for righteous conduct. The humble shared the divine life; the poor were blessed in spirit, for theirs was the kingdom of Heaven. Love was the secret of individual blessedness and held the promise of social salvation. Love and good will toward all men was the basic principle for complete fulfillment. That person was blessed who conducted himself so as to add to the glory of God and the welfare of mankind. Eternal salvation could in this way be achieved. On the other hand, evil toward another human being, no matter how humble he may be, was a defiance of His righteous will and made one unfit for His kingdom. "All things, therefore, whatsoever ye would that men should do unto you; even so do ye also unto them: for this is the law and the prophets." Love toward men enjoined one to refrain from anger, resentment and bitterness. Acts and even thoughts of unkindness and hate toward others were to be eschewed, since, in their violating the spirit of Love, they were no different than overt acts of murder. "Ye have heard that it was said of them of old time, Thou shalt not kill; and whosoever shall kill shall be in danger of the judgment; but I say unto you, that every one who is angry with his brother shall be in danger of the judgment; and whosoever shall say to his brother, Raca, shall be in danger of the council; and whosoever shall say, Thou fool, shall be in danger of the hell of fire. If, therefore, thou art offering thy gift at the altar and there rememberest that thy brother hath aught against thee, leave there thy gift before the altar and go thy way, first be reconciled to thy brother, and then come and offer thy gift." Monogamy and fidelity were to be rigidly maintained: "Ye have heard that it was said, Thou shalt not commit adultery; but I say unto you, that every one that looketh on a woman to lust after her hath committed adultery with her already in his heart. And if thy right eye causeth thee to stumble, pluck it out, and cast it from thee; for it is profitable for thee that one of thy members should perish, and not thy whole body be cast into hell. And if thy right hand causeth thee to stumble, cut it off, and cast it from thee; for it is profitable for thee that one of thy members should perish, and not thy whole body go into hell." Divorce was a confession of Love's failure. "It was said also, Whosoever shall put away his wife, let him give her a writing of divorcement; but I say unto you, that every one that putteth away his wife, saving for the cause of fornication, maketh her an adulteress; and whosoever shall marry her when she is put away committeth adultery." Essential was a yielding to those who sought to divert one from the goal of Love for all men. "Ye have heard that it was said, An eye for an eye, and a tooth for a tooth; but I say unto you, Resist not him that is evil, but whosoever smiteth thee on thy right cheek, turn to him the other also. And if any man would go to law with thee, and take away thy coat, let him have thy cloak also. And whosoever shall compel thee to go one mile, go with him twain. Give to him that asketh thee, and from him that would borrow of thee turn not thou away." One should love one's enemies and seek to convert them from evil to Love. "Ye have heard that it was said, Thou shalt love thy neighbor, and hate thy enemy; but I say unto you, Love your enemies, and pray for them that persecute you, and ye may be sons of your Father which is in heaven; for he maketh his sun to rise on the evil and the good, and sendeth rain on the just and the unjust. For if ye love them that love you, what reward have ye? do not even the publicans the same? And if ye salute your brethren only, what do ye more than others? do not even the Gentiles the same? Ye therefore shall be perfect, as your heavenly Father is perfect." The temple of God that was man's body was not to be desecrated by evil thoughts and deeds. The individual could achieve the greatest good by acting with God for the good of man. Wealth was not important. "Lay not up for yourselves treasures upon the earth, where moth and rust doth consume, and where thieves break through and steal; but lay up for yourselves treasure in heaven, where neither moth nor rust doth consume, and where thieves do not break through nor steal, for where thy treasure is, there will thy heart be also." "Therefore I say unto you, Be not anxious for your life, what ye shall eat, or what ye shall drink, nor yet for your body, what ye shall put on. Is not the life more than the food, and the body than the raiment? Behold the birds of the heaven, that they sow not, neither do they reap, nor gather into barns; and your heavenly Father feedeth them. Are not ye of much more value than they? And which of you by being anxious can add one cubit unto his stature? And why are ye anxious concerning raiment? Consider the lilies of the field, how they grow; they toil not, neither do they spin; yet I say unto you, that even Solomon in all his glory was not arrayed like one of these. But if God doth so clothe the grass of the field, which to-day is, and to-morrow is cast into the oven, shall he not much more clothe you, O ye of little faith? Be not therefore anxious, saying, What shall we eat? or, What shall we drink? or, Wherewithal shall we be clothed? For after all these things do the Gentiles seek; for your heavenly Father knoweth that ye have need of all these things." Through proper prayer one could find reward: "Ask, and it shall be given you; seek, and ye shall find; knock, and it shall be opened unto you, for every one that asketh receiveth; and he that seeketh findeth; and to him that knocketh it shall be opened. Or what man is there of you, who, if his son shall ask him for a loaf, will give him a stone, or if he shall ask for a fish, will give him a serpent? If ye then, being evil, know how to give good gifts unto your children, how much more shall your Father which is in heaven give good things to them that ask him?" God, the Spirit of Love, came to him who worshipped reverently. By adoring his holy name, Love invaded the heart; it bestowed a beneficence of strength and honor, it forgave baseness, frailties and failing. "Our Father which art in heaven, Hallowed be thy name. Thy kingdom come. Thy will be done, as in heaven, so on earth. Give us this day our daily bread. And forgive us our debts, as we also have forgiven our debtors. And bring us not into temptation, but deliver us from the evil one." Love bades to forgive baseness, wickedness and evil. "For if ye forgive men their trespasses, your heavenly Father will also forgive you. But if ye forgive not men their trespasses, neither will your Father forgive your trespasses." Modesty, self-denial and humility were virtues. "Blessed are the poor in spirit; for theirs is the kingdom of heaven. . . . Blessed are the meek; for they shall inherit the earth. . . . Blessed are they that mourne; for they shall be comforted. . . . Blessed are they that hunger and thirst after righteousness; for they shall be filled. . . . Blessed are the pure in heart; for they shall see God. . . . Blessed are the peacemakers; for they shall be called the children of God."

Later religious values; the cardinal virtues. The right in Christian theology to interpret divine revelations as recorded in the sacred scriptures brought out many beliefs which were regarded as heretical, but which ultimately resulted in revisions in the doctrines, as, for example, those that were brought about by the Gnostic heresies. Interpretations by Augustine (340-397) and Ambrose (340-397) of the four cardinal virtues of Christian wisdom as consisting of God as its highest truth; Christian fortitude as resisting the seduction of fortune and fighting steadfastly against evil; Christian temperance observing measure and humility in conduct; and Christian justice as sharing the earth with man's brethren for common benefit formed the basis of later systematic ethical theories. The concept that one could be exculpated from guilt even for a wrong act if his motive was good brought Abelard (1079-1142) to the Council of Sens. However his principle was later accepted to the effect that the consequences of an act were considered less important than the motive behind it. The Franciscan theologian Bonaventura (1221-1274) avowed that, through grace, a man's latent virtues could be activated. However the perfect beatific vision could come only in the next life. The emphasis on faith was epitomized by Anselm (1033-1109) in his statement: "He who does not believe will not experience, and he who has not experienced will not understand." Reason's duty was to affirm the truth of what faith makes us believe.

A more extensive delineation of the role of reason was elaborated in the teaching of Thomas Aquinas (1225-1274) the principal force in Scholasticism, who, reviving Aristotelian ideas of happiness as being proportionate to the degree of contemplation of truth, contended that the intellect is immortal and godlike, and is supported by man's supernatural desire for the vision of God toward whom reason directs his life. Roger Bacon (1220-1292), pursuing the philosophy of Aristotle as well as that of Seneca, impounded reason as a force that drove man toward affiliation with the Infinite. All ethical argumentations required a rhetorical rather than scientific basis. Opposing the primacy of reason, however, were a group of medieval philosophers, namely Duns Scotus (1266-1308) and William of Occam (1300-1347), who insisted that will could not be truly free of it were chained to reason. A struggle developed among opposing groups on the basis that the Aristotelian ideas of virtue conflicted with true Christian standards. Disagreement also revolved around the meaning of humility, particularly in its relationship to the asceticism that it sponsored. Important was the introduction into this polemic of Jewish writings, particularly those of Maimonides (1135-1204) who preached a perfection born out of enjoyable living, intelligence, bodily health and the moral virtues of courage, generosity, moderation and modesty. During the middle ages also a mystical element permeated Christianity in which the ecstatic vision of Plotinus was merged with the Christian doctrines of love. So intense was this drive toward Neoplatonism that an open breach with the church was threatened.

Quasi-legal approaches to morality. The philosophic interests of Scholasticism receded in the fourteenth and fifteenth centuries in favor of a quasi-legal approach to morality during which manuals were developed, listing questions and proper answers, for the conduct of auricular confession. This systematic casuistry resulted in the application of a penal jurisprudence for thoughts and acts that were considered improper. However because there was after the death of Boniface VIII no strong authority to judge the validity of rules of behavior, which were as disparate as the authorities who issued them, people were tempted to seek out those authorities whose contentions supported their own desires for a relaxation of moral rule. The Jesuits, champions in the struggle to uphold the Catholic church that was being threatened by the Reformation, accommodated themselves to the growing revolt in the theory of "Probabilism" which forgave a layman during confession and held him guiltless for opinions that he gleaned from aberrant authorities since he knew no better. The confessor was enjoined to produce a "probable" opinion in favor of the layman if it would unburden the conscience under his charge.

The Reformation, initiated by Martin Luther (1483-1546) who, trained in the Church of Rome as an Augustinian friar, ostensibly in revolt against the Pope for the sale of indulgences, but more likely prompted by a struggle with his own conscience ("I was shaken by desperation and blasphemy of God," he wrote in 1527), exalted God's word as expressed in the Scriptures, promoted the simplicity of Apostolic Christianity, preached the right of private judgement in opposition to ecclesiastic authority, and upheld individual responsibility for the human soul before God rather than papal dictation of purgatorial punishments. Faith was restored as the vehicle to eternal life, and to counteract the inherent corruption of human nature, absolute obedience to Christian duty was imperative.

Humanistic values and standards of social duty. Restoration of quasi-legal platforms for morality was, during the seventeenth century counteracted by the drive to formulate an independent philosophical basis for the moral code, which embodying Platonic, Aristotelian and Stoical forms, found expression in a new humanism which was even more resisted by the representatives of the Reformation than such paganism had been opposed by the Roman hierarchy during the Renaissance. A new moral philosophy emerged independent of Catholic and Protestant suppositions, which was poignantly expressed by Sir Thomas More (1478-1535) in his *Utopia*. The promotion of a morality of this world detached from Christian revelation was supported by the revelations of modern physical science which was at the time in its dawn.

The breakdown of ecclesiastical authority and the separation of Church from State coincided with a period of religious wars which left secular communities isolated whose moral relationships to each other required moral coding. The most systematic attempts at this were executed by Gentilis (1557-1611) and especially by Grotius (1583-1645) in his treatise *De jure belli et pacis.* Recognizable a priori was natural law, an aspect of divine law, that promoted man's tranquil association with his fellow creatures. Thus it promoted "natural" impulses for marital fidelity, the keeping of promises, the living together of individuals and families in peace, the recognition of human equality, justice, equity and parental responsibility. These principles, presumably derived from the nature of man, governed all human societies. Grotius did not assume that these laws could not be violated by man, however he contended that such violations were in opposition to man's rational and social nature. A search for the sources of these natural tendencies toward orderliness in human relationships involved many philosophers.

In England, Hobbes (1588-1679), under the influence of Epicurus and Bacon, proposed a materialistic psychology to the effect that all of man's impulses derived ultimately from bodily wants toward self-preservation and toward the pursuit of pleasure. His self-centered philosophy regarded pity for others as the imaginings of a similar calamity befalling oneself; the detached admiration of the beautiful, an anticipated "pleasure in promise;" the absence of immediate pleasure seeking, a hiatus in which power was sought for future pleasures. Reason provides the means for pleasure and self-preservation. Rules of moral and social behavior are maintained only insofar as they fulfill pleasurable and self-preservative functions. Government serves only as a common power to enforce by law and institution the observance of rules for the common pleasure and self-preservation of its citizens. Though man is not unconditionally bound to moral behavior, it is to his advantage that he abide by precepts of good faith, prohibition of contumely, equity, etc. Social peace and order are contingent on the acceptance of this morality of social duty.

Hobbes' contributions, which created a new trend in philosophic thought, were challenged by Cumberland (1631-1718) in his *De legibus naturae,* who contended that laws of nature centered in the divinely sanctioned supreme principle of the "common good of all," a concept later developed in universal utilitarianism, and particularized by Cudworth (1617-1688) in his treatise on *Eternal and Immutable Morality*. This considered man as a rational being who strove for good for its own sake; good and evil were independent of will or desire, human or divine.

Intuitive values. These formulations were more explicitly elaborated by John Locke (1632-1704), the founder of English empiricism, who, agreeing with Hobbes that "good" was equated with pleasure in man's mind and "bad" with pain, labeled things "morally good" which were associated with rewards and things "morally bad" those tinctured with punishments. Ethical rules could be obligatory, independent of political society and were subject to scientific construction on principles that were intuitively known. Intuition as a principle value was also a factor in Spinoza's philosophy. According to Spinoza (1632-1677) the self-preservative and other instincts powered "passive emotions" and supported certain uncritical beliefs. These uncontrolled drives fostered a kind of human bondage from which escape was possible only through reason and rational control. True understanding resolved hate and fear and was the means to peace of mind, and to positive "active emotions." The highest form of value was intellectual development that terminated in "intuitive knowledge," which, once achieved, enabled the individual to contemplate the universe as a unity and to achieve a oneness with and love for the Absolute Being.

Early utilitarian values. Reconciliation of the social and personal selves was the striving of Shaftesbury (1671-1713). Man, he alleged, can be understood only in relation to society as a whole. We can call this nature "good" if his motives and actions contribute to the good and happiness of the larger system of which he is a part. The hierarchial structuring of individual happiness from egoistic to altruistic objectives established benevolence and the welfare of others as equivalent to moral goodness, the highest value in human aspiration. Shaftesbury's *Characteristics,* published in 1713, brought about a focusing in English ethical thought from abstract rational principles to an introspective study of the interplay of impulses and sentiments. While Descartes and Locke had developed similar themes, Shaftesbury was first to promote psychological experience as the basis of ethics, an inspiration that influenced Butler, Hutcheson and Hume and became a structure on which later utilitarianism was mounted.

Butler (1692-1752) supporting Shaftesbury in the contention that social drives were no less natural to man than self-preservative impulses, insisted that pleasure was not their primary aim, but the mere result of their fulfillment. Harmony between prudence and virtue, the natural appetites, self-love and social interests was the function of a duty enlightened mind. Consciousness was a cognitive force that passed judgement on man's motives and self interests. One may see in Butler's view a revival of Plato's idea of human nature as constituted by a regulated community of impulses as well as a topological sectioning of the mind into natural, self and moral constituents. Hutcheson (1694-1746) also pointed out the regulating and controlling function in the body's economy of the moral sense and stressed both personal excellence and benevolence as equally worthy and superior drives.

In his *Treatise of Human Nature,* and *Enquiry Concerning the Principles of Morals,* David Hume (1711-1776) inveighed against the sovereignty of reason in the kingdom of behavior considering it merely the means of perceiving the order of things to which passions and actions were not necessarily subordinated. Through inductive reasoning Hume assumed some common principle in the different elements of personal merit, for instance in "discretion, caution, enterprise, industry, frugality, economy, good sense, prudence, discernment" as well as "temperance, sobriety, patience, perseverance, considerateness, secrecy, order, insinuation, address, presence of mind, quickness of conception, facility of expression." What they had in common was their utilitarian service to the individual. Moral sentiment, like benevolence, he declared, can become a motive to action "only when it gives pleasure or pain, and thereby constitutes happiness or misery." Reason "is no motive to action . . . [except to direct] . . . the impulses received from appetite or inclination." Moral imperatives were directly related to personal interest or happiness, an aspect of which was sympathy with the pleasure of others. Adam Smith, in his *Theory of Moral Sentiments* in 1759, added to this the idea that an aspect of human nature was the pleasure that a person experienced when he realized that his feelings are in accord with others. Man valued that which brought approval from his fellow humans.

The supreme value of personal pleasure (Egoistic Hedonism) was revived by Jeremy Bentham (1748-1832) into a system of ethics somewhat related to, but not identical with those of his contemporaries, Price, Reid, Drigold Steward, Whewell and Paley. Man, according to Bentham, was dragooned into accepting as an index the values of the greatest number under the sanction of law, public opinion and religion. This promotion of utilitarian principles as a ranking standard was supported by John Stuart Mill (1806-1873) who added to Bentham's sanctions those of inner social feelings which were also, by the "Law of Association," related to pleasure or pain, even though it revealed itself in loving "virtue as a thing desireable in itself." In 1748 Hartley published *Observations on Man,* which originated an associational theory by an elaborate exposition of how the pleasures and pains of "imagination, ambition, self-interest, sympathy, theopathy, and the moral sense" develop from elementary sensations of pleasure and pain. His ideas remarkably resemble those of Pavlov who established the laws of classical conditioning.

The value of duty.　A reconciliation of moral values with the materialism of science was the object of many philosophers including Kant (1724-1804). As a rational being, said Kant, man was bound to the inborn "categorical imperative" of duty. The "goodness" of an act, was to be judged by the motive behind it, a chief motive, being *duty* which must be performed for duty's sake. The force behind any act must be the reasoned conclusion that one was behaving on the premise of duty. Perhaps the greatest duty was to strive for the happiness of others. As an instrument of reason, man had the responsibility for reason's perfection in himself rather than for the promotion of pleasure. Happiness would follow as the reward in the wake of his fulfillment of duty. The rightness of a dutiful prompting was to be judged by its universalization: "Act only on such a principle as you can, will should be a universal law." Thus a proposed action was moral if the agent was prepared to will that it should become universal law. It was to this point that Hegel (1770-1831) applied himself. Agreeing that morally duty was to be valued for duty's sake, Hegel argued that people could follow contradictory courses out of these ideas of duty that could be ascribed by them to universal law. The *content* of the act, insisted Hegel, was a valid judgement of its moral worth. It had to be in harmony with the laws, customs and institutions of the society in which the individual lived. The ideal morality was a consonance of subjective with objective social values.

Evolutionary ethics. Like a colossus the empirical sciences were beginning to tower over all fields of learning including philosophy. Darwin (1809-1882), postulating a continuity with animal forebears, considered that man's moral qualities were essentially an extension of his instinctual drives which had survived in the struggle for existence. The social tendency, he contended, originally an instinct rooted in parental or filial affection, through natural selection had continued to fashion morality in its more complex forms. Herbert Spencer (1820-1903) was a strong advocate of evolutionary ethics insisting that it is "the business of moral science to deduce from the laws of life and the conditions of existence what kinds of action necessarily tend to produce happiness." However, Spencer was unable to dissociate himself from formal philosophy sufficiently to achieve this objective, nor to distill scientific criteria out of data issuing from the biological sciences. Efforts to concoct an evolution of morality from conditions of animal existence proved themselves to be a failure.

It was Nietzsche (1844-1900) who made the greatest contribution to evolutionary principles in morals. To Nietzsche brute strength and cunning were key traits in the struggle for existence. The Christian virtues of compassion for the poor, weak and suffering were merely an essential passing stage in the evolution of the Übermensch (superman). This stage was to be superceded by survival of the strong and vigorous, since the weak were not equipped by nature to endure in the fight for survival. Altruism was consequently to be abandoned, peace to be deprecated; war was the great purifier filtering out the strong. The Christian virtues of chastity, humility and selflessness, and the "slave virtues" of industry and regularity, were to be replaced by values of courage and cruelty. Men, however, should sacrifice their personal interests for the highest good of a society which, dedicated to restore aristocracy to its rightful domain over slaves, would conquer, with terror and violence, other societies weakened by the infirmities of Christianity.

Later utilitarian values. Opposing the growing empiricism which was invading the field of ethics were the British Idealists, Green (1836-1882) and Bradley (1846-1924). Green, professing that the self could never be the object of scientific understanding, put the highest value in directing the will toward social good, such as public welfare and utility. Bradley, in his *Ethical Studies,* written in 1876, stressed self-realization in both social and non-social dimensions as the preferred moral force. There were also those like August Compte (1798-1857) who continued to stress the uniqueness in man of social feelings, his dedication to others being the highest in the scale of human values and the prime source of his happiness. Compte alleged (1) that societies passed through evolutionary changes which influenced their institutions, customs and habits; (2) that man could be understood only through knowledge of his past history; and (3) that moral and political ideals could not be approached through purely abstract and unhistorical methods. Rather they could be determined through an understanding of "social dynamics."

A morality was proposed that rose above the interest of the self toward fulfillment through concern with other selves. This utilitarianism, developed in the writings of Sidgwick (1838-1900) and Moore (1873-1958) assigned moral supremacy to those actions which brought about the greatest intrinsic good. Benevolent motives, stressed Moore, were praiseworthy, but were not equivalent to actions that resulted in good. Summer (1840-1910) ascribed to society the arbitrary function of assigning good to any action it considered proper at a particular moment. Westermarck (1862-1939) in his *Ethical Relativity* pointed out that values were relative to both the valuing person and the society in which they operated. Moral judgements were, he claimed, issued to virtues by social sanctions. These sociological theories of ethics in turn brought forth criticisms on the basis that the "right" could not simply connote what society approved. Amidst these arguments a number of other systems were evolved including pragmatism and logical positivism.

Pragmatic values. William James (1842-1910), C. S. Peirce (1839-1914)) and John Dewey (1849-1952) contributed the skeleton and flesh of pragmatism, a viewpoint that bases its judgement of values on the premise that man's reasoning powers are directed at manipulating the environment to gratify his inner needs. The essence of truth in thinking or moral reflection does not lie in naked, objective fact, or in a static independent reality, but in the overcoming of obstacles and practical problems that impede adjustment. Truth consists of what works. Conflict of values that prompt diverse actions results in moral problems, necessitating moral deliberations to resolve conflict, in the face of which Dewey, who called his theory "Instrumentalism," advised a consideration of the practicality and consequences of each opposing value. Needs on which values depend can be studied empirically. A choice is considered right that results in a solution of the conflict, but such a choice does not establish its absolute rightness or goodness since auxiliary conflicts may eventuate. Human nature is in evolutionary flux and consequently no everlasting *summum bonum* can be established; however the harmonious satisfaction of the self and others can be proposed as a basis for "right" conduct with the understanding that no universal rules are possible. Dewey's influence was felt chiefly in the field of education. The rejection of objectivism in pragmatic philosophy, and the feeling that truth is related to fact and not to the notion that it is practically useful mobilized criticism from philosophers such as Bertrand Russell.

Empirical values of logical positivism. In the 1920's, inspired by Ludwig Wittgenstein's book *Tractatus Logico-Philosophicus,* which dealt with a new theory of meaning, a group of mathematicians in Vienna organized what became known as the "Vienna Circle" to discuss the validity of approaching all knowledge through language forms common to all science. To their movement they assigned the name "Logical Positivism" which, in essence, purported that moral judgements unsubstantiated by empirical evidence could not be accepted as true even though they sometimes proved in personal experience to be functionally useful. Value directives reflect emotional rather than cognitive attitudes and require analysis in terms of their linguistic meaning. Many of the formulations of the Vienna Circle were published in the journal *Erkenntnis* and, when members of the group came to the United States, in the *International Encyclopedia of Unified*

Science. Ludwig Wittgenstein established his residence in England and was a potent force in promoting Logical Positivism in that country. This philosophy gained a great deal of popularity in 1936 through A. J. Ayer's book, *Language, Truth and Logic.* The hope was to demonstrate a unity of science, with a reduction of all concepts to physical terms with elimination of purposive or teleological ideas.

Logical positivism contends that reality cannot be adequately delineated because of limitations in language. Accordingly, philosophy, in posing questions about reality, is unable to respond with the proper answers, since no verification is possible except through the methods of science. Philosophy can, however, involve itself in the analysis and clarification of language through the use of symbolic logic. True propositions are those so framed that they cannot be denied ("doctrine of tautology"). However, since ordinary communication permits of no exact formulations, an artificial language may have to be constructed to cover all rules. The meaning of any statement may be determined by the method of its verification. Experimental evidence is needed to establish the truth or falsity of the conglomorate single facts ("atomic propositions") that constitute a derivative hypothesis ("verification principle"). Because communicating individuals employ a common syntax, they are able to transmit structures ("forms") of meaning even though their experiences ("content") may be divergent ("doctrine of form and content"). Empirical propositions may be verified, but only by statements of a singular and fundamental kind ("protocol statements") which, when made logically, establish the truth ("doctrine of protocol statements"). Since value statements express mere attitudes, they cannot be verified or reduced to any factual terms. They are hence without meaning. Logical Positivism has found faithful devotees especially among scientists and logicians; however the verification principle, the mainstay of Logical Positivism, while applicable to natural science, is now considered to be too deficient and restrictive to deal with many aspects of ideation, such as values.

Existentialism. Existentialism is a philosophy that has attracted many psychotherapists in Europe and the United States, who have, on its premises, developed "ontological" or "existential" treatment procedures which attempt to combine psychotherapeutic and philosophical doctrines (Tillich, 1952; May, 1950, 1959; Binswanger, 1947, 1956; Boss, 1957; Frankl, 1948). More or less, existentialism is oriented around the writings of Søren Kierkegaard (1813-1855) who revolted against the impotence of Hegel's philosophy of "pure thought" as a means of coping with the paradoxes and contradictions of human existence (Kierkegaard, 1951). Fruitless, contended Kierkegaard, were faith and coercive divine grace, proffered as a means of salvation; Christ was no substitute for true experience in the world. Nor was science of any greater use, for man's search for facts as an escape from moral decisions was not possible. Haunted by perpetual despair and dread (Angst, anxiety) which "eats away all the things of the finite world and lays bare all illusions," man could not remain a mere spectator, finding refuge in evanescent comforts. He was forced to assume responsibility and to make a choice for himself. Duty might dull his consciousness; it might, in a romantically optimistic way, enable him to evade responsibility. However it could not eliminate man's responsibility. Essential was a free choice to which the individual committed himself as a whole in the recognition that human values were insignificant indeed. In the crisis of existence, the only true refuge was a leap into religion in which man related to the infinite. His freedom of choice was a fount of anguish because he had a limited time in which to act. He needed courage to be. When his immortal soul was at stake, his choice would crucially determine which way to turn.

Kierkegaard, being a religious man, stressed the choice of religion as a means of surcease from anguish. Later existentialists, however, made other choices, such as agnosticism (as in the writings of Jean Paul Sartre) or aestheticism. Karl Jaspers, in *Man in the Modern Age* considered that the chief threat to modern man may lay in our complex technology. *Philosophie,* published in 1932, spoke of the importance of man's persistent quest for knowledge as a means of actualizing himself. In 1927, Martin Heidegger, pupil of Edmund Husserl, the originator of phenomenology, wrote *Sein und Zeit* which followed Husserl's feeling, as expressed in his *Logische Untersuchungen* that man needed to focus on his inner experience as a way of apprehending the outer world. Heidegger detailed some of the important inner experiences underlying our scientific understanding. His description of the preoccupation of man with the inevitability of death had a profound influence on existential formulations.

Periods of crisis in world history, such as during and after war, bring forth the philosophy of protest against the world. Various interpretations of existentialism have been made by different devotees of this philosophy. Jean Paul Sartre stresses the need to preserve human loneliness from the encroachment of others. Karl Jaspers and Gabriel Marcel emphasize the interpersonal communication of "loving conflict" during which each participant retains his uniqueness. Other prominent existentialists who have contributed to the theory are Karl Barth, Martin Buber, Emil Brunner, Paul Tillich and Reinhold Niebuhr.

Values of mysticism. Mysticism possesses properties which have led a number of psychotherapists to explore its therapeutic potentials, some even attempting to blend mystical formulations into their treatment systems, as, for instance, Zen Buddhism (Watts, 1957; Ben Avi, 1959; Suzuki, 1957). The mystical striving is two-fold: first, there is an attempt to achieve communion with the Absolute (the Highest, the One, God, Brahma, the Order of Heaven, Being of beings) and, second, a desire to grasp through introspection the ultimate nature of reality.

The Absolute is conceived of in various symbolic forms as an encompassing, irresistible indwelling power that can overcome the temporal, the changing, the relative, the impermanent and other aspects of existential anxiety. The Absolute establishes stability, methodical arrangement and permanence in the universe. Since it is impossible to approach it through the senses, the establishment of the Absolute is attempted by epistemological arguments, by mandates in sacred writings presumably divinely inspired and enforced through religious discipline, and by mystical experience.

Immanuel Kant (1724-1804) attacking traditional metaphysical arguments that reality is behind external appearances, insisted that the human mind was so constructed that it could deal only with what comes to it through the senses, and was experienced by the "phenomenal self." Though inaccessible to reason as well as the senses there was an Absolute, a "Thing-in-itself," which, the source of the effects in the world of appearances, could be experienced as an aspect of the "noumenal self" when man acted in accordance with the moral law, the core of ultimate reality at the center of being. Ficht (1762-1814) developed the idea of the noumenal self as an "Absolute Self" the source of man's identity, a concept elaborated by a number of other philosophers who avowed that our limited powers restricted the possibility of knowledge of the inner self. Hegel (1770-1831) comparing this limitation to "a night in which all cows are black," applied himself to an elucidation of the Absolute. This, he said, was composed of an inactive principle existing both in nature and in mind. Nature was the medium in which the Absolute works out its logical schemes in terms of space and time.

Approach to the Absolute through mystical experience has an older and more elaborate history. In such experience there is no need for intermediaries, such as oracles, priests, historical revelations or prayers; rather direct and personal contact is made, resulting in an identification and fusion with the Absolute substance. Description of the austerity of mortifications suffered, of the rapture of visions, of the intoxication of the senses as the soul finds its resting place with the Absolute have produced some of the world's most florid and poetic literature. The mystical experience may become a part of multiform religious or philosophic systems. Historically it has become organized into bodies of practice among dissatisfied adherents of inflexible, formalistic and legalistic religions who seek to detach themselves from the ossification of formulas and ceremonies toward a liberating union with a divine spirit.

A search for the Absolute has preoccupied philosophers and theologians throughout the ages. Its most prominent forms have been found in Eastern systems, for example, the Brahmanic and Buddhist religions which promoted the illusory nature of reality and the goal of absorption in mystical essences toward ecstatic enlightenment ("nirvana," "satori"). Reduction of the self to plastic passivity as a precurser to the transcendental experience was encouraged by sets of rules outlining contemplative and ascetic rituals which resulted in a deadening of the consciousness and in the promotion of self-control, including the mind and various physiological functions.

Mystical expressions were part of the contemplative asceticism of the Essenes of Judaea. Among the Alexandrian Jews, Plato's speculations were employed in the Logos or Divine Sophia which preached reflective meditation, resignation and complete submission to divine spirituality. Neoplatonism permeated the systems of the Greeks during the third century, most vividly represented in the teaching of Plotinus, and preached the value of repudiating reality with transcendence of material existence, suspension of reason and liberation from the bondage of the senses toward a state of higher revelation and "enthusiasm." Sufism, a mystical practice among the Persians in the ninth century, established the unity in nature and the joy inherent in beauty and love, ideals sensualized later by Mohammedan adherents.

The writings of Dionysius the Areopagite (which incidentally were later proved forgeries) exerted a profound influence on medieval Christian thought. Essentially neoplatonic, they purported that the divine source transmitted the sublime transcendence of power and guidance through meditating beings (angels) unto men. Love flooding from God drew its own creations to itself. Mysticism became gradually fused with dogma. It opposed the scholasticism of the period which proposed acceptance by reason of truths independent of rational grounds, as, for instance, through revelation. Religious truth was external to the mind; mystical truths were inherent within the individual and not subject to external authority. Bernard of Clairvaux (1090-1154) claimed that ecstatic visions of the divine were the reward of the deadening of the senses. "To lose thyself in some sort, as if thou wert not, and to have no consciousness of thyself at all—to be emptied of thyself and almost annihilated—such is heavenly conversation. . . . So to be affected is to become God." Under the influence of Hugh of St. Victor (1096-1141), the anti-dialectical trend continued, mystic contemplation becoming entrenched as a value, which, with the growing reaction against formalism, found its strongest expression during the twelveth to fourteenth centuries in German mysticism. Wars, famines, floods and the black death tended to focus religion inward and closer bonds united people. The Society of Friends of God was organized at this time. A speculative, contemplative mysticism which followed the ideas of Meister Eckhart (1260-1327) became popular. Jan van Ruysbroeck, Gerhard Groot, Johann Tauler, Thomas Munzer, Caspar

Schwenkfeld, and Sebastian Franck practiced and preached their own special brands of mysticism. During the seventeenth century George Fox founded the Quakers whose meditative practices toward experiencing the "inner light" and the influence of the Spirit were of mystical direction.

Philosophical mysticism during the seventeenth century appeared under the banner of the Cambridge Platonists and the Boehmenists. Henry More, Pierre Poiret, William Law, Johann Scheffler, Lucie Christine, Charles de Foucauld, Maharshi Devendranath Tagore, and Sadhu Sundar Singh have all contributed to the rich literature of mysticism.

Present-day mysticism resembles with little variation its older forms. In all systems direct personal experience is approached through mystic states in which the individual becomes aware of his oneness with the Absolute. By various stages the mystic achieves this union. Through meditation the student invokes his reason, memory and will, focusing on some scene or subject. He may, in western religious systems, employ a preparatory prayer for Grace, focusing on several points in the image he creates, then pouring his devotion out freely into the Colloquy. In Eastern systems, he may attempt to suspend his reason, employing certain aids, such as breathing and body control, as in Yoga; or practice of the arts, like archery or flower arrangement in Zen Buddhism; or indulge asceticism to bring the body under control, to extinguish desire and reduce the self to submission. Gradually reason gives way to inner contemplation, and even to hallucination. Excitement, rapture, despair, and varied other emotions may develop within the matrix of a delicious solitude.

A symbolic dialect unites mystics of all persuasions. In different words there is described the same adventure: the "paradox," of existence, the "journey" into the unknown within, the periods of "darkness" and "light," the excitement and enlightenment at achieving the strange and wonderful world of inner reality, the "marriage" with the Absolute or Divine.

Conflicts between science, psychotherapy and religion. Two centuries before Christ the historian Polybius decried the religion of the Romans: ". . . my view is that it has been done to impress the masses. . . . All that can be done is to hold them in check by fears of the unseen and other shams of the same sort. It was not for nothing, but with deliberate design, that the men of old introduced to the masses notions about gods and views of the after life. The folly and heedlessness are ours, who seek to dispel such illusions." Freud, in his "The Future of an Illusion," considered the major religious ideas "patently infantile" and "incongruous with reality." He considered fealty to God a childish prompting to perpetuate the relationship with a protective parental figure. The fact that science was unable to provide answers to all reality did not in Freud's opinion justify recourse to religion: ". . . science is no illusion. But it would be an illusion to think that we can get elsewhere what science cannot give."

Psychotherapy and religion, however, are not really at war. They share a number of common goals. They both strive to bring about better self understanding and a full utilization of latent creative potentials. Psychotherapy attempts to do this by bringing the person to a fuller realization of himself in terms of his past experiences and the residual distortions that hamper his present interpersonal relationships, while encouraging new and more productive behavioral patterns. Religion encourages the search for new meanings by affiliation with the divine being, and by worship and prayer which can suffuse the human spirit with hope, with strength to resist deviant drives and with new directions that will lead to self-fulfillment. Both psychotherapy and religion seek to alter destructive motives in the individual and to lead him toward humane values that will accomplish the greatest social good, such as honesty, loyalty, charity, love, courage and compassion for suffering. Both psychotherapy and religion promote salutory family and community relationships as virtuous to the highest degree.

There are, however, certain conflicts that exist among the disciplines of science, psychotherapy and religion (Freud, 1949; Jung, 1933; Reik, 1951). A good number of devotees of science admit that there are aspects beyond observable experience, but they are not willing to relegate these to a deistic substance or being in whose transcendent vision all phenomena are clear. Religion resents the implication of some scientists that the craving for God is an infantile or neurotic prompting, and it challenges the denial of the validity of an Almighty Being, since science can offer no experimental proof that there is none. What better evidence is there for God, protests religion, than the miracle of creation of living things, the source of which no scientist has been able to qualify, let alone quantify. On more specific grounds a point of conflict between psychotherapy and religion is that the former regards moral deviation as a symptom, the latter as a sin. Psychotherapy is apt to look on man as an irrational entity, and on deviations as unwilled and manipulatory of man without his desire or awareness. Religion considers man a rational being, and holds deviation to be an act against man and God to be judged in moralistic terms. It suspects psychotherapy of belittling man's responsibility for his behavior, appeasing his guilt feelings and encouraging the acting out of errant impulses and drives that are morally reprehensible. Thus anger, covetousness, envy, gluttony, lust, pride and sloth—the seven deadly sins—are acquitted as by-products of an individual's past conditionings, the liability for their present manifestations falling on the shoulders of parents and not patients. Moreover psychotherapy is considered by some representatives of religion to encourage a closer relationship to the psychotherapist than to the pastor, even diverting patients from seeking spiritual guidance. Psychotherapy counters by pointing out that certain religious precepts contradict the biological nature of man, that a literal interpretation of the Bible will cast a shadow over healthy urges that stir in all persons in the course of personality development; for instance, in relation to sexual and aggressive feelings. Relegating the individual to eternal damnation for sexual drives out of wedlock, for adulterous thoughts and fantasies, for interest in prurient materials, for retaliatory aggression in the face of humiliation or exploitation, for rebellious impulses toward parental agencies, serves merely to mobilize pathological guilt and shame, to sponsor masochistic, sadistic and other neurotic responses, and even to cripple healthy drives for reproduction and self-defense. The meek, the poor, the sad, the peaceful are not necessarily blessed. Temporary anger, resentment and bitterness may be justified and need not irreparably violate the spirit of Love. Mutilation is not a worthy punishment for phantasies that oppose monogamy and fidelity. Passive compliance cannot always be the response to those who promote evil, nor can one in the spirit of tolerance always love one's enemies.

There are some psychotherapists who believe that any morality which proposes an absolute code, violation of which brings supernatural punishment, contains within it seeds of conflict, since the definition of what constitutes the proper morality is open to some question. Thus obedience to authority and unquestioning submission conflicts with self-determination and independence. Unworldliness with its abandonment of natural pursuits leads to passive alienation; shame and guilt in relation to body desires may inspire monastic self-torment and degradation of sexual desire with a repression of rage and aggression. Many of the sacrificial rituals in religion stem from this conflict. Religious systems, it is also claimed, may sponsor conflict and bad values, representing the bad in the form of an inhabitant of the underworld—devil, satan, Baal-Zebub—an evil representative who opposes God for the mastery of the universe. This struggle, recorded vividly in the Talmud and New Testament, and especially in the Apocryphal and Apocalyptic Books, is literally incorporated in the conviction that the devil is constantly on the alert to occupy man's body and to pervert him to his satanic purposes. This is a potent fount of anxiety, particularly when the religious individual feels incapable of living a perpetually sainted life. More in the form of an abstract idea than in a pictorialized image of a cloven-footed, horned monster, the notion of an invasive devil may preoccupy those whose fundamentalistic notions are rooted in medieval conceptions that continue to be a means through which they control and discipline themselves.

A conflict in moral values may furthermore be sponsored in religious systems that conceive of the right and ability on the part of the individual to do and think as he wishes as theologically opposed to the idea of predestination. If we conceive of man as "free," we must assume an autonomous morality with self-determinism and unpredictability dissociated from divine foreknowledge. Volumes were written attempting to reconcile this apparent dilemma, and bitter debates raged about free will and predestination during the Dark and Middle Ages as well as the Reformation. Notable was the dispute between Pelagius and Augustine, during which the liberal Pelagius, asserted that after all God could be forgiving of man's independent propensities since He was not an unmitigated tyrant. Augustine countered with the idea that there was no inconsistency in believing both in human freedom and in divine foreknowledge, since Adam did possess the freedom of choice between good and evil. However in his voluntary preference of self to God, Adam chose evil, which guilt all later men were justly condemned to perpetual absolute sinfulness and punishment, unless they chose God's unmerited grace to share the benefits of Christ's redemption. Psychotherapy claims that sources of behavior are too often considered by religion to be the product of moral judgements of which the individual is fully aware and which he may freely "will," and "choose" and control. Very often, however, the determining factors in behavior are unconscious in nature, outside the awareness and control of the individual. He is frequently driven in his choices by forces that are not apparent to him at moments of decision. A view reconciling these disputations, and one which psychotherapy endorses is that moral choice is still man's in his freedom to exercise it; however, he has the nature to misuse it. Awareness of his unconscious enables him better to exercise moral control. Freedom of will does not imply capriciousness or irresponsibility. This mitigates but does not resolve the conflict.

Another conflict brews over the matter of fundamentalism. A believer must accept the divine authorship of scripture, since the authors were merely the agencies for the transcription of sacred and unalterable doctrines. Deviation from the sentence and word, in the mind of fundamentalists, tends to discredit God. Science contends that the bible is a human document subject to the same kind of study and analysis as any other human document. Fundamentalists insist that biblical criticism, and the pointing out of discrepancies in the scripture, are illusions of the Devil. Some attempt at reconciliation of scientific and religious concepts was made during the eighteenth century by assigning to the Great Architect of the Universe the First Cause, from which point the world took off on its own. With the introduction of the Darwinian doctrines of evolution, the cosmological references in the Bible underwent a great challenge; the fundamentalists erecting an even firmer platform of faith quoting the words attributed to St. Anselm: "All truth by whomsoever uttered, is from the Holy Spirit." Can one's intellectual integrity stand up to so strong a feeling of faith? Reconciliation of the opposing viewpoint is often attempted by the judgment that while the ideas in the Bible are divine, the canons of scripture are the product of the Church on earth. A strong undercurrent of fundamentalism still exists that may disturb those who have an investment in orthodoxy. Fundamentalistic conflict incidentally is not confined to the Bible; it invests may fields of thought, even scientific, where allegiance to the omniscience of founders of a movement tends to circumscribe one's thinking to the letter of published text or to interpretations of the text by self-appointed prophets.

Application of values to personal adjustment. One of the problems in philosophy, which proposes to posit ideals and ultimate values, is that a search is made by its practitioners for a unitary principal, a universal essence, that constitutes truth of the highest order. Over and over it is demonstrated that the multiple dimensions of the universe and its human inhabitants make it impossible to assign to any one value any real primacy. The individual operates with a multitude of values that fluctuate with his social role, the state of his physiological homeostasis, the level of his anxiety, and other forces both within and outside himself. We must conclude that there is never a permanent supreme "good," but rather that there are many "goods" that gain a functional ascendancy at different periods. Thus the average person may at one time operate with "Christian" and at another with "pagan" values; his reasoning powers may dominate the scene at a certain stage, and, at another, his biological promptings; his self interests will alternate with social impulses that put the welfare of other persons at the fore. Certain thoughts, feelings and acts that promote anxiety-relieving coping mechanisms and defenses will, for the moment, be treasured commodities, only to be relinquished when security and self-esteem are enhanced. A host of derivative values will cluster themselves around some immediate purpose or need, only to be discarded and replaced with new standards when their purpose has been fulfilled. The sacrificing of oneself tc a great cause and the dedication of one's life to noble pursuits of patriotism, humanitarianism, honor, justice, charity and other benefactions are but one face of the value coin, the reverse of which may reflect egocentricity, self-indulgence, cruelty, pusillanimity and avarice.

There are times when the individual will be swayed by the standard of seeking his personal happiness (*Egoistic Eudaemonism*) in the form of physical pleasures (*Hedonism*) or pleasures of the mind (*Epicurianism*) intellectual or aesthetic, which lead him toward artistic and spiritual ideals. In pursuit of future happiness in heaven, he may exploit ascetic aims or dedicate himself to religion with sacrificial ferver. There are periods when the happiness of his community will be the most important objective (*Universalistic Eudaemonism* or *Utilitarianism*), or the promoting of the happiness of others at the expense of his own (*Altruistic Eudaemonism* or *Altruism*). The "highest" value may consist for the moment in a striving toward a full development of his latent potentialities. Here the individual may, at varying times, pursue his own personal development (*Egoistic Perfectionism*), the evolution of a "perfect" community or society (*Universalistic Perfectionism*) or the fulfillment of others around him (*Altruistic Perfectionism*). He may operate with the idea that the sense of "duty" constitutes the highest good, that "right" is judged by the obligation that inspires it, rather than by its results. It will be seen then that man is moved not by one supreme value (*summum bonum*), but by a host of values conditioned by his inner biological needs ("id values?") drives for self-actualization ("ego values?"), and moral promptings ("super-ego values?").

It is interesting that, in organizing his values, modern man often exploits philosophical systems that parallel those developed hundreds and even thousands of years ago. Thus he may consider the "well-balanced" personality as one which regulates itself according to four cardinal virtues: (1) *temperance* which makes for the ability to control appetites in accordance with reason; (2) *fortitude* which helps to gain mastery over impulsiveness; (3) *wisdom* in employing one's resources in an expeditious way; and (4) *righteousness* which permits harmonious integration of all aspects of the individual toward a unified whole. Happiness may also be sought in a productive existence devoted to the interests of others and the comprehensive welfare of society. Unfortunately, emotional distortions tend to divert the individual from these formulas, which were originally fashioned by Plato and Aristotle, that advocate a life of moderation, courage, intellectual sagacity, virtue and social good, toward the exploitation of values that serve neurotic aims.

Hedonism may be commandeered as a credo to give sanction to impulses for unbridled pleasure seeking. In conditions, such as psychopathic personality, alcoholism, drug addiction and sexual perversion, a doctrine that endorses pleasure as a mainstay of life may lend patronage to an irresponsibility that is prompted by uncontrollable inner needs. Epicurianism may be espoused as a means of balancing an incubus of guilt in persons with consciences that refuse to lend sanction to life's delectations without restraint. Worries are purged from the mind as wanton waste, with encouragement of (1) regulation of one's life to anticipate unpleasant events so that they may be avoided; (2) arrangement of matters so that as much pleasure as possible may be crowded into each day; (3) elimination of those pleasures for which one has to pay too dearly; (4) judiciously cutting off of thoughts that mobilize pain or create tension; and (5) banishing profitless recriminations about the past or anticipated fears of the future. The conduct of an Epicurian existence is pursued as John Stuart Mill has tersely stated it: "Pleasure and freedom from pain are the only things desireable as ends; and all desireable things are desireable either for the pleasure inherent in themselves, or as means to the promotion of pleasure and the prevention of pain."

In the canons of Stoicism the detached soul often finds refuge, embracing its injunctions as did the Roman stoic Seneca many years ago: "All life is bondage. Man must therefore habituate himself to his condition, complain of it as little as possible, and grasp whatever good lies within his reach. No situation is so harsh that a dispassionate mind cannot find some consolation in it. . . . Apply good sense to your problems, the hard can be softened, the narrow widened, and the heavy made lighter by the skillful bearer." External circumstances are never considered good or evil in themselves; they are to be judged by the effect they wield on the mental life of man. Physical pain may inspire a person to achieve greater personal courage and equanimity. A humiliating circumstance may heighten one's dignity as he exerts his efforts to rise above it. In the words of Epictetus: "Men are disturbed not by things, but by the view which they take of things.

Thus death is nothing terrible else it would have appeared so to Socrates. But the terror consists in our notion of death, that it is terrible. When, therefore, we are hindered, or disturbed, or grieved, let us never impute it to others, but to ourselves; that is, to our views." By coating himself in a protective stoic cloak, the individual may then learn to endure hardship with equanimity and joy.

As a personal philosophy, Scepticism is also rooted in man's search for tranquility. If the quest for knowledge, understanding and truth brings on stress and pain, why struggle for that which is probably unattainable? By scrupulous doubting, and withdrawing into the self, the individual may attempt to escape unhappiness. In the effort to avoid any dogmatic statement about anything, he may extend his doubting both to his ability and his inability to know. This is a prime defense in the obsessive-compulsive who may, like Sextus Empiricus, operate under the idea that no statement can be true because "if it is true, it is false, and, if it is false, it is true. All arguments and counter-arguments balance each other."

Diametrically opposed to the values of Scepticism are those of dogmatism, which, as a defense, may be exploited for inner harmony and peace of mind. This is the sanctuary of a severe and authoritarian conscience that seeks constant control because of a devastating fear of uncertainty and the unknown. The sceptic is fired by values to avoid the controlling hand of fate. By doubting he negates it and liberates himself from the shackles of cosmic doom. The dogmatist seeks to mold fate to his own controlling designs. It may be seen then that the value of certainty and truth, and the need for a precise structuring of reality in the dogmatist, and the value of doubting in the sceptic, that negates certainty and structure, are both manifestations of obsessive-compulsive personality structures and constitute different modes of coping with precisely the same kind of anxiety.

The individual, reared in a religious atmosphere, or achieving a decision through a need for personal salvation, may at times dedicate himself to the adoration of God, either as a symbol of power and protectiveness, or in the form of ethical self-devotion; for instance, as a Christian in the morality embodied in Jesus

Christ. He may then conceive that what appeals to his soul as deserving of worship is what he feels his soul may trust which has the ability to deliver him from evil, sin, fear and death. In this way he will, according to his interpretation, attempt to conform to the purpose of the life of his Saviour, with expressions of devotion to God and love for his fellow men in accordance with the theological creeds and sacraments, and in the church, synagogue, temple or mosque within which he finds his identity. Those aspects of religion which possess greatest meaning will be cherished by him whether they involve ritual, sacrament, logic, belief, faith, or the privileges of church membership. The values for the individual will be contingent on his needs and range from the comforts of group belongingness to the enhancement of the spiritual aspects of the self and the enrichment of moral goals. This is not to say that neurotic objectives may not be sought through the exploitation of religion's instrumentalities; for religion, with its Divinities, ceremonies, dogma and taboos offers the neurotic individual rich resources for the projection of strivings, demands and defenses that keep him in psychological homeostasis.

On the other hand, the values of science may become for the individual, at least temporarily, of supreme importance in supplying answers to the ultimate meaning of life and reality. He will then extrapolate from the data of his observations the functional relationships between pertinent variables in the hopes of bringing some order to the phenomenalistic chaos that invests his life. Through the doorway of empiricism rather than faith, he will approach purpose and meaning. And yet he will, realizing the limits of reason, attempt from time to time to liberate himself from the tyranny of his senses by introspection and subjectivism.

Transcending the empirical sphere into the hazardous world of speculation, some men become traitors to reason. Accepting the dictum that "things may not be quite other in themselves than that which by the laws of our thought they necessarily appear," concepts are welded together by the irrational force of faith. In quest of experience beyond knowledge, they penetrate into the penumbra of mysticism. Justifying their illusions of reality, they argue that man is limited by the testimony of his senses. Perspectives of reality are always relative to the percipient. No universal standard exists or can exist except that which each man discovers by retreating into himself. Liberated from the fetters of his reason, he can blend himself with the Absolute and then perceive the ultimate nature of reality. His mind, he may believe, is directly linked to the Cosmic Mind, which All-seeing and All-knowing can fashion his destiny and direct his journey through infinity from gloomy evil toward the luminous fields of spirit, love and truth. It is to be expected that the mystical path to tranquility is the refuge of souls who are unable to brook the harsh realities of their existence, whose coping mechanisms have failed them or who have lost their faith in the dignity of humanity and the virtue and safety of the material world.

Organization of one's life around philosophic, religious, or for that matter, "scientific" values are inescapable aspects of mental functioning. They are woven into the complex tapestry of adjustment. They may be adapted, changed or discarded as the shifting needs of the individual dictate modification.

A natural question is how do we judge values? Three solutions pose themselves. First, we may believe that standards of good and evil, right and wrong, exist independent of actual experience, a rationalistic, *a priori* viewpoint, repeatedly proposed by philosophers like Socrates, Plato, Aristotle, Spinoza and Hegel. Second, we may assign "good" or "bad" to man's immediate capacity to apprehend intuitively the ultimate value of things. Finally, we may empirically consider that values are "good" or "bad" relative to the basic biologic and social needs of the individual, a point of view that is gaining ascendancy among psychotherapists.

The question of moral sanction also enters into the problem of values. What constitutes the sense of duty that enjoins men to do certain things and not others? Is it, first, the anticipation of happiness from fulfillment of certain acts? Is it, second, outside authority who espouses certain values and whose good will the individual seeks or whose reprimand he wishes to avoid? In the latter case we may distinguish the authorities and differentiate their sanctions. Thus religious sanctions uphold moral imperatives as commands of God; political sanctions support certain legal activities and condemn illegal ones; social sanctions sponsor customs and traditions. Or is it, third, the internalized representative of authority, the conscience that metes out rewards and punishments? Our clinical judgment tells us that all three types of sanctions are operative.

XIII

Field Theory; Gestalt Theory; Ecology

THE NEWTONIAN CONCEPT OF THE PHYSICAL UNIVERSE, WHICH supported the notion of simple forces acting between one body and another in a fixed framework of space and time, was, around the end of the 19th century, replaced by the idea of energy in a material system determined by the configuration and motion of that system. Chiefly through the experiments of Faraday it became apparent that the universe could best be envisioned in terms of fields under the influence of electromagnetic forces which existed apart from any material particles within the fields. Einstein and Infeld (1938), in a brilliant exposition, pointed out that what was really significant for the description of physical phenomena was not the charges in the field or the particles, but the field itself: " . . . the field *here* and *now* depends on the field in the *immediate neighborhood* at a time *just past* . . . " A field, they insisted, could be particularized by observation of how a body acted within that field.

These physical formulations were eagerly seized upon by other disciplines to explain the mutual interdependence of phenomena, toward evolving ways of "analyzing causal relations and of building scientific constructs" (Lewin, 1951). A basic assumption was that no event is explicable except in terms of its relationship to the total configuration of events of which it was a component part.

Among the groups who contributed to the integration of these concepts in the behavioral sciences were the Gestalt theorists, Kohler, Wertheimer and Koffka, who regarded random sensations as fused into a single unitary perception by a number of mental operations that could not be explained by introspection or mechanical laws of association (Koffka, 1935). Indeed, they felt that the introspective dissection of an experience into its component parts was disruptive in effect. A phenomenologic way of

looking at human behavior was much more serviceable, particularly conceiving it as a dynamic fusion of field forces and wholes,
the sum of which alone could not explain the final assemblage.

According to Gestalt theory, physiological laws govern how the
individual *perceives* things in time and space. Perception is the
property of the perceiving organism in whose brain a physiological configuration occurs identical in form ("isomorphic") with the
perception configuration of the initiating stimuli. The form
things assume have a "whole character" that is more than a mere
aggregate of all its parts; a microscopic analysis of constituents
of a total experience is therefore not meaningful. The "whole
character" of experience can best be explained in terms of field
forces, i.e., influences acting upon each other constantly; their
resultants effectuating change in the consummate state. This
makes for great flexibility in the experienced configuration. Trans-
formations and transpositions are inevitable. There is, however,
nothing chaotic about this process, since restraining ("bounding") features operate to maintain good form and to achieve a
cohesive organization.

Another important figure who contributed substantially to
"field theory" was Kurt Lewin (1936, 1951)). Lewin embodied
in his psychological formulations such concepts from physics as
"force," "tension," "fluidity," etc., although he insisted that
psychological phenomena could be delineated only in psychological terms. According to Lewin the individual operated within
a psychological field occupying one region of "life space" on which
he was dependent and which in turn was dependent on him.
Attracting him ("positive valence") were other regions through
which the person had to pass in his journey through life, traversing
resistances or "barriers." Unattractive regions had a "negative
valence" for him, promoting conflicts as he went through them to
reach his goal. Forces of positive and negative valences encouraged or impeded locomotion through life space. Perception of
specific valences and the structure of life space permitted the
prediction of behavior. This necessitated an understanding of
the individual's personal ways of viewing the universe. Psychological events were determined by the totality of transactions of
the individual within his life space, and by mutual intertwinings
of all the functional systems that constituted the person as a

whole. Psychological reactions, consequently, could be approached only in relation to concrete environmental situations. Without analysis of their interdependent relations to the total situation, psychological events were vitiated abstractions. A dynamic equilibrium existed in the comprehensive system that constituted man, a change in one aspect immediately producing compensating changes in other aspects. Thus tensions issuing from needs initiated a setting of goals, and stimulated goal directed activities toward the release of tension. Lewin attempted to organize his ideas of vectors in the individual's life space in terms of mathematics, one such effort resulting in a geometric arrangement that he called "hodological space" (Lewin, 1938).

The impact of the work of the Gestalt theorists and of Kurt Lewin on psychology has been substantial. While some of their formulations have been criticized, the conceptualization of the individual as an atom in the molecule of the world, and of his constituent parts in interdependent balance have led to an emphasis on systematic correlations of patterns of organization, and a focusing on interplay and interaction in human behavior, extending from the unitary bodily cell to the most complex social institutions. Thus the individual cell may be regarded as a complex homeostatic device of numerous structural organelles including membranes, microsomes, ribosomes, Golgi apparati, lipoprotein granules, mitochondria, nucleoli, nuclei and chromosomes bathed in a solution of ions, organic complexes, water matrices, organic complexes, enzymes, clathrates and chelations (Leake, 1965). Each of these parts functions contingently on the others; it is not their simple juxtaposition that is responsible for the vital activities of the living cell, but their patterning (Weiss, 1962). Principles of organization enter into the combination of molecules into aggregates, of cells into tissues, of tissues into organs, of organs into systems. Individuals are interdependent on other individuals; populations of organisms on their ecological environment.

Dynamic organization is the essence of ecology which contends that all parts of the total environment act on one another so that changes in one part will effect changes in the whole. Of concern to man is how human communities and societies adapt to their environment, particularly the technological systems and modes of social arrangement which foster his survival needs. Ethnographic, geographic and demographic data bring out the consociation of many factors; for instance, population growth, spatial patterns of economic activity, social division of labor, and regional distribution and variation in disease and death rates. Gradually emerging has been the concept that societies reflect environmental and demographic conditions and that there is a close interconnection between populations, technology, social groupings and the environment. For example, as technology becomes more sophisticated, the ecological factors of increased food supply and abundant shelter resources support aggregations of population in urban communities; as economic surplus accumulates beyond minimum existence needs, specialized social roles become more possible. Human behavior then is dependent on the physical and technological basis of group living, as well as on the social substructure as influenced by the environment. A study of the spatial patterning of such social phenomena as mental illness, delinquency, divorce, forms of family organization and distribution of ethnic groups has brought out many affiliated factors. Within cities, for instance, it has been determined that slum areas have the highest incidence of deviant and criminal behavior, such as crimes of violence, juvenile delinquency, alcoholism, drug addiction, physical and mental disabilities, prostitution and severe mental illness (Berelson & Steiner, 1964).

Field theoretical ideas, entering into our modern concepts of personality functioning, have an important signification for psychotherapy. Thus we may regard any single behavioral act as a Gestalt of countless molecular units—physical, psychological and social. Accordingly, the individual's social transactions cannot be dissociated from his intrapsychic and physiological transactions. Motivation, dealt with as an entity apart from the totality of physical and social experience, is impalpable. To attempt this is to manipulate a disembodied part, interesting in its composition, but meaningless in terms of consummate organismic functioning. The impact of environmental forces on the perceptual apparatus, the selective filtering of stimuli by the neocortex, the collocation and fusion of information through cognitive processes, the emotional toning by subcortical structures which impart to experience an affective meaning, the directive pressure of inner biological needs, the somatic stimulation of liberated bodily chemicals, the releasing of fixed motor patterns, the activation of purposeful muscular movements, and finally, the subjugation of the total assembly of responses to inner value influences and to cultural and social pressures; all this, sometimes within a fraction of a second, makes for a complex synthesis of behavior that can be explicated only in molar terms.

Each link within the total reactive chain will affect the workings of the other links and, ultimately, the operations of the total chain. We may illustrate this by the phenomenon of sensory deprivation. Continual perceptual inflow has been shown to be essential for proper mental functioning (Hebb, 1958). Deprived of such stimuli, normal subjects may develop visual hallucinations, mood disorders and delusions similar to those that appear in LSD intoxication (Bexton et al, 1954; Lilly, 1956). Disturbances, therefore, in any of the constituent parts of man will have profound effects on all of his other articulations, and on his functioning as a whole. Disruption of total integrative activity may be brought about by pathology in any segment of the physiological, psychological, social and spiritual continuum. Thus biochemical dusturbances will reverberate in intrapsychic and behavioral pathology. Value conflicts may have their counterparts in social, interpersonal and visceral upheavals.

On the other hand, restoration of healthy operations in any one disorganized and disorganizing division will tend to exert a healing influence on the other divisions. Somatic therapy, by restoring the physiological equilibrium, may prove salutary for every other area of functioning. Psychological therapy commonly registers its beneficial effects in restored physical health and social rehabilitation. Environmental treatment may make a constructive imprint on the total well-being. Spiritual guidance commonly supports and brings solace to the physiologically sick, psychologically distraught and socially disorganized, leading to tension reduction and the restoration of a sense of mastery. Each of the zones of man is thus intricately and inseparably fused with the other, contributing to both his diseased and healthful dispositions.

XIV

Practical Applications
and Future Prospects

IT HAS BEEN THE THESIS OF THIS BOOK THAT MAN, FROM ENZYME reactions to spiritual promptings, exhibits a unification of function subject to general laws of nature and laws seemingly unique to himself. The subsystems constituting man—*physical* (physiological, chemical), *psychological* (intrapsychic), *social* (interpersonal) and *spiritual* (philosophic, religious) have traditionally been approached through special models each of which deals with circumscribed phenomena in their assigned zone. Attempts to generalize from any one model to subsystems other than its own have resulted in muddle. This has given rise to hopes that it may some day be possible through a refinement of communication to arrive at a universal scientific language that permits a pooling of information from the various biological, psychological and sociological fields. Through the eventuating consolidation of concepts there may then emerge a general systems theory which allows for the integration of the different subsystems, and a synthesis of findings in man with those in other open systems. One of the earliest efforts in this direction was instituted in the late 1920's by Ludwig von Bertalanffy (1950 a, b), who, with Anatol Rapoport and Kenneth Boulding evolved some interesting postulates which were elaborated later by James Miller and Ralph Gerard into a more structured form. A spreading interest in a general systems theory has encouraged the development of an interdisciplinary and multidisciplinary Society for General Systems Research in which psychiatrists and psychologists are playing an important role. The ultimate objective is the formulation of a theory that can harmonize the different theoretical approaches in the field of human behavior. For the present, however, it must suffice to deal with separate models, and the foregoing chapters have described some of the important contributions to psychotherapeutic theory and practice of affiliated fields.

Along the wide spectrum of approaches to the human being innovated by these fields—physiological, biochemical, psychological, sociological and philosophical—psychotherapists of diverse persuasions have clustered themselves, many affirming their specialized focus as the best solution for problems of an emotional nature. Chart V outlines the principal fields affiliated with psychotherapy, the professional identities of the chief workers, and the treatment methods that these fields sponsor.

Information from fields affiliated with psychotherapy has many practical applications for the psychotherapist. From neurophysiology we may gain an understanding of the mechanisms of emotion, the bodily responses to stress, the nature of the recording of memories, the biology of sleep and dreaming, the functions of selected brain areas, and the dynamic interactions of the neocortex, reticular system, limbic system and hypothalamus. Such information helps to organize a rationale for the somatic therapies. From biochemistry we gain percipience of how the energy resources of the body are governed, the role of enzymes and neurohormones, the chemical regulation of brain metabolism, the mechanisms of mood formation and psychoses, and the influence of drugs on specific areas of the brain. This provides a basis for the employment, where essential, of the psychoactive drugs during phases of psychotherapy when depression, excitement, schizophrenic disorganization or intense anxiety interfere with the psychotherapeutic process. Genetics supplies leads on how hereditary influences may interfere with proper metabolic operations within the brain, rendering some individuals more susceptible to psychological disorders. Behavior genetics yields clues regarding the ubiquity and uniqueness of inherited response patterns among different individuals and their potential modifiability through learning. Ethology points out the role of fixed neuromuscular coordinations in man that are operative normally, or that are released during neurotic or psychotic adaptations. Conditioning theory forms a structure for knowledge of how personality organization evolves, higher and lower brain structures interact, and disorganizing and maladaptive behavior is learned. It supports a premise for comprehending the behavior therapies.

CHART V

APPROACH	PRINCIPAL FIELDS INVOLVED	AFFILIATED PROFESSIONALS	TREATMENT METHOD
Biological	Neuroanatomy, Neurophysiology, Neurology, Biochemistry, Ethology, Genetics.	Neuroanatomists, Neurophysiologists, Neurologists, Geneticists, Physiologists, Biologists, Biochemists, Ethologists, Physicians, Nurses.	Somatic Therapies: drug therapy, sleep therapy, electroconvulsive therapy, insulin coma, psychosurgery (topectomy, lobotomy)).
Psychological	Conditioning and Learning Theory, Developmental Theory, Personality Theory, Psychoanalytic Theory.	Psychiatrists, Psychologists (experimental, educational, developmental, clinical); Educators; Psychiatric Social Workers.	Psychotherapy, Psychoanalysis, Behavorial Therapy, Therapeutic Counseling, Hypnotherapy.
Sociological	Social Theory, Role Theory, Field Theory, Ecology, Cultural Anthropology, Group Dynamics.	Sociologists, Social Workers, Social Psychologists, Anthropologists.	Casework, Environmental Therapy, Group Therapy, Psychodrama, Sociodrama, Family Therapy, Social Therapy, Transactional Therapy.
Philosophic	Religion, Philosophy.	Clergymen, Philosophers.	Existentialism, Zen Buddhism, Yoga, Religious Therapy.

Data from animal experimentation, principally the development of experimental neuroses and their removal by various stratagems, introduce avenues for approaching human neurosis. A grasp of the dynamisms of stress and adaptation are vital for discernment of what has happened to the neurotic individual whose coping mechanisms no longer keep him in homeostasis. Developmental and personality theories, which essentially deal with ontogenetic maturation, occupy the cynosure of the psychotherapist's interests, since he will arrange his hypotheses around forces in the patient's life that have shattered his adaptive potentials. Learning theory grants a foundation for studying the acquisition of disorganizing habit patterns; it introduces principles which, incorporated in the therapist's interviewing procedures, may help facilitate the therapeutic process. Psychoanalytic theory—Freudian, Ego-analytic and Neo-freudian—presents the therapist with a rich body of formulations that delineate conscious and unconscious intrapsychic operations, subsidizing a systematized methodology. It also opens views to the therapist of his own irrational emotional projections toward the patient (counter-transference). Social theory and role theory are viable systems for the understanding of social process and interpersonal conflict as a means toward environmental and casework approaches. Group dynamics delineate tactics of altering attitudes and patterns through interaction. Anthropology illuminates the cultural atmosphere that shadows the patient's attitudes and responses toward the therapist's personality, methods and goals. Philosophy enables the therapist to appreciate the power of value conflicts, and apprises him of the need for altering value systems in his patient that prevent the expression of basic needs. Communication and information theories focus the therapist's attention on problems that are expressed through altered symbolic functioning. Finally, field theory permits a perspective of neurotic problems in relationship to environmental, interpersonal, intrapsychic and physiological variables, as well as a gauge of therapeutic goals in terms of the broadest social objectives.

The widening horizons of psychotherapy, encouraged by contributions from its affiliated fields, reflect new directions experienced in many other areas of science (Berelson, 1963). The steam engine model for the creation and disposal of energy, popular in the days of Freud, no longer applies to the nuclear age. The idea of a limited amount of energy available to the individual, which exhausted the reserve for defense mechanisms at the expense of growth and learning, is no longer tenable. The nuclear energy model assures that the energy input is greater than any amount of energy that can possibly be consumed. Many implications derive from this axiom.

Gaining increasing acceptance is the conception of function and structure as dynamically interrelated within a field of forces that range from the remotest regions of the environment to the innermost recesses of the organism. A reverberating chain of reactions takes place involving electronic, biochemical, neurophysiological, psychological, social, cultural, and spiritual elements. In this never-ending transactional feedback among and between the different constituents, the individual develops his personality structure in all of its cohesiveness and uniqueness. Newer data coming from behavior genetics, psychology, anthropology and sociology also indicate that our traditional concepts of unmodifiable maturational laws which lead to set structures and patterns are giving way to ideas of flexible behavioral constellations that are significantly influenced by experiential factors in the cultural and social milieu. Even our conventional idea of intelligence as a genetically fixed trait is being replaced by a new notion of the modifiability of intelligence through stimulating or depriving factors in the environment which operate to change the intelligence quotient even into old age (Gordon, 1965).

The studies of Piaget (1951, 1952, 1961) on the intellectual growth of children, and with Inhelder, (Piaget and Inhelder, 1958, 1964) on changes in logical thinking from childhood through adolescence have contributed much to our understanding of stages of cognitive development. Other investigations also point to the great importance of cognitive processes involved in learning, problem solving, and the development of language and its function in thought (Vygotsky, 1962). Possessing within himself the capacity for organization, the child incorporates stimuli from his environment selectively, choosing components for assimilation which become the building blocks of his personality. During the complex interactions between the child and his environment, dynamic impacts on each other are registered. The child learns to accommodate himself to those aspects of the environment that he cannot change. Flexible elements of the environment are molded to the child's needs. Cognitive structure is the product of these processes of assimilation and accommodation. Satisfactory development is contingent on an environment that provides ample opportunities for the essential processes of assimilation and accommodation.

Among our changing concepts are deliberations regarding the immutability of most aspects of development. Through propitious learning and conditioning even fixed motor patterns may undergo alteration. Instead of regarding the individual as one whose destiny is more or less shaped by genetic and other biological forces, some of the newer information points to functional relationships among the many fragments that constitute man's being. The inspiration of the individual as a self-actualizing system who seeks to fulfill his creative needs is replacing the idea of man as a machine who is principally motivated by deprivation. Rewards are inherent in activity and mastery for its own sake, not merely to gratify urgent needs.

Psychotherapeutic methodologies have been influenced by these changing impressions, reflected in alterations in treatment goals and stratagems. From the conventional dyadic, long-term model of therapy geared toward "insight," we see explorations into various kinds of group approaches, the joint treatment of married couples and entire families, conditioning procedures aimed at specific symptoms, milieu manipulations which may extend to the structuring of an entire therapeutic community, and the combined employment of psychotherapy with somatic treatments. Short-term therapy, directed at both abbreviated and reconstructive goals, is being encouraged by expanding insurance coverage for emotional illness. The preoccupation with intrapsychic content is being supplemented with a consideration of the interpersonal transactions that are occurring within the therapeutic situation, exploring the varying roles the patient is playing with the therapist and others. The laboratory of the psychotherapist is being extended into the community, fostering the working in a consultative capacity with various professional persons who deal with problems of people on a broad level; for example, educators, law enforcers, clergymen, physicians, dentists, and lawyers. Community mental health has become as vital to the interests of society as is individual mental health, and this has necessitated the acquisition of new knowledge and skills regarding the social and cultural networks that envelop people and institutions. Finally, the psychotherapist has been interesting himself increasingly in philosophy, particularly the world of values; how these are developed, and their psychological function. Accordingly, he may adopt formulations from certain philosophical systems and blend them with his therapeutic techniques. In this context he is becoming increasingly aware of cultural forces as they influence the value orientations of his patients as well as his own, and the need to deal with these forces as part of the therapeutic task.

The ultimate effect of these trends and trajectories is toward a reasoned eclecticism. Eclecticism does not presuppose a disordered conglomeration of disparate devices thrown together into an expedient pot pourri. Rather it involves the selection and studied amalgamation of aspects from varied sources that are compatable with and reinforce one another. In this way a fusion of concordant doctrines is implemented which buttresses up weaknesses in the individual systems. The synthesis, harmonious as it may seem for the moment, is subject to constant reorganization as new ideas and methods make themselves available. Unfortunately eclecticism has come to connote unprincipled and even counterfeit opportunism practiced by those who sacrifice integrity of doctrine for temporary rational consistency. The uncritical syncretism characteristic of the ancient philosophic sect of Eclectics does not apply to the present-day eclectics, although purists and formalists are apt to consider their thinking too loose and unsystematized. On the whole the eclectic direction has proven a refreshing diversion from the rigid, oracular and dogmatic schools and systems some of whose members refuse to compromise their position under the mistaken conviction that if they are not God's chosen people, they are at least his principal scientific missionaries.

The eclectic orientation is complemented by a need on the part of the therapist for closer collaboration with members of other professions. A shift in philosophy and attitude of the mental health worker is required before a pooling of knowledge and skills can be properly accomplished. The traditional role of the psychotherapist is an isolated one operating as he does in his own little orbit outside the range of other bodies in the behavioral solar system. To shift his orbit will require an opening of his mind to the worthwhileness of the contributions of workers in the other fields and a willingness to respect their position on a parity with his own. For only in this way can the proper interdisciplinary cooperation come about that can bring new vistas to psychotherapy with a true enrichment of its potentials.

REFERENCES

ABEL, T. M.: Cultural patterns as they affect psychotherapeutic practices. Am. J. Psychother., 10:728-739, 1956.

—: Cultural contexts and psychotherapy. Paper read at the Postgraduate Center for Mental Health, Oct. 12, 1965.

ABRAMSON, H. A.: Lysergic Acid diethylamide (LSD-25):III. As an adjunct to psychotherapy with the elimination of the fear of homosexuality. J. Psychol., 39:127, 1955.

ALEXANDER, F.: Psychosomatic Medicine, Its Principles and Applications. N. Y., Norton, 1950.

—: Psychoanalytic Contributions to Short-term Psychotherapy. In: Short-term Psychotherapy. (Wolberg, L. R. Ed.) N. Y., Grune & Stratton, 1965.

— & FRENCH, T. M. et al.: Psychoanalytic Therapy, N. Y., Ronald Press, 1946.

ALLPORT, F. H.: Social Psychology. Boston, Houghton, Mifflin, 1924.

ANGYALL, A.: Foundations for a Science of Personality. N. Y., The Commonwealth Fund, 1941.

APPEL, K. E.: Religion. In: American Handbook of Psychiatry. Vol. II (Arieti, S., Ed.) N. Y., Basic Books, Pp. 1777-1782. 1959.

ARIETI, S.: Some basic problems common to anthropology and modern psychiatry. Amer. Anthrop. 58:26-29, 1956.

ASERINSKY, E., & KLEITMAN, N.: Regularly occurring periods of eye motility and concomitant phenomena during sleep. Science. 118:273-274, 1953.

— & —: Two types of ocular motility occurring in sleep. J. Appl. Physiol. 8:1-10, 1955.

BALES, R. F.: Interaction Process Analysis; a Method for the Study of Small Groups. Cambridge, Mass., Addison-Wesley, 1950.

—: Small group theory and research. In: Sociology Today: Problems and Prospects. (Mertin, R. K., Broom, L., & Cottrell, L. S., Jr. Eds.) N. Y., Basic Books, Pp. 293-305, 1958.

BALES, R. F., HARE, A. P., & BORGATTO, E.F.: Structure and dynamics of small groups: a review of four variables. In: Review of Sociology: analysis of a decade. (Gittler, J. B. Ed.) N. Y., Wiley, Pp. 391-422, 1957.

BANKS, S. A.: Psychotherapy: values in action. In: Behavioral Science Contributions to Psychiatry. (Regan, P. F. & Pattishal, E. G., Jr. Eds.), Boston, Little, Brown & Co., 1965.

BAVELAS, A.: A mathematical model for group structure. Applied Anthrop. 7:16-30, 1948.

—: Communication patterns in task-oriented group. In: The Policy Sciences; Recent Developments in Scope and Method. Stanford Univ. Press, Pp. 193-202, 1951.

BELL, D. A.: Intelligent Machines. N. Y., Blaisdell Co., 1962.

BELLAK, L. & SMALL, L.: Emergency Psychotherapy and Brief Psychotherapy. N. Y., Grune & Stratton, 1965.

BELLO, F.: The tranquilizer question. Fortune, Pp. 162-166. May, 1957.

BENDER, L.: Psychopathology of Children with Organic Brain Disorders. Springfield, Ill., Thomas, 1956.

BEN-AVI, A.: Zen Buddhism. In: American Handbook of Psychiatry. (Arieti, S., Ed.) N. Y., Basic Books, Pp. 1816-1820, 1959.

BENEDICT, R.: Patterns of Culture. Boston, Houghton, Mifflin, 1934.

179

BENJAMIN, J. D.: The innate and the experimental in child development. In: Lectures in Experimental Psychiatry. (Brosin, H. W., Ed.) Pittsburgh, Univ. of Pittsburgh Press, 1961.

BERELESON, B. (Ed.): Behavioral Sciences Today. N. Y., Basic Books, 1963.

— & STEINER, G. A.: Human Behavior. N. Y., Harcourt, Brace & World, P. 608, 1964.

BERGMAN, P. & ESCALONA, S.: Unusual sensitivities in very young children. Psychoanal. Stud. Child. 3/4:333-352, 1949.

BERNE, E.: Transactional Analysis in Psychotherapy. N. Y., Grove Press, 1961.

BEXTON, W. H., HERON, W. & SCOTT, T. H.: Effects of decreased variation in the sensory environment. Canad. J. Psychol. 8:70, 1954.

BIANCHI, L.: The Meccanica del Cervello e la Funzione Dei Lobi. Frontali, Forino Bocca, 1920.

BINSWANGER, L.: Ausgewählte Vorträge und Aufsätze. Bern, Francke, 1947.

—: Existential analysis and psychotherapy. In: Progress in Psychotherapy. (Fromm-Reichmann, F. & Moreno, J. L., Eds.) Vol. I, N. Y., Grune & Stratton, 1956.

BION, W. R.: Group dynamics; a re-view. In: New Directions in Psychoanalysis. (Klein, M. et al. Eds.) N. Y., Basic Books, Pp. 440-447, 1955.

BOARD, F., PERSKY, H. & HAMBURG, D. A.: Psychological Stress and Endocrine Functions. Psychosomat. Med. 18:324-333, 1956.

BOAS, F.: General Anthropology. Boston, Heath, 1938.

BONNER, H.: Group Dynamics; Principles and Application. N. Y., Ronald Press, 1959.

BOSS, M.: Psychoanalyse und Daseinanalytik. Bern, Huber, 1957.

BOSZORMENYI-NAGI, I. & FRAMO, J. L. (Eds.): Intensive Family Therapy. Theoretical and Practical Aspects. N. Y., Hoeber Medical Division, Harper & Row, 1965.

BOWLBY, J.: Maternal Care and Mental Health. Geneva, World Health Organization, 1952.

—: The nature of the child's tie to his mother. Int. J. Psychoanal. 30:1-24, 1958.

BRACELAND, F. J.: Clinical psychiatry today and tomorrow. In: Faith, Reason and Modern Psychiatry. N. Y., Kenedy, 1965.

BRIDGER, W. H.: Signaling systems in the development of cognitive functions. In: The Central Nervous System and Behavior. (Bazier, M. Ed.) N. Y., Josiah Macy, Jr. Foundation, Pp. 425-461, 1960.

BRIFFAULT, R.: The Mothers. N. Y., Grosset and Dunlap, 1959.

BURGUM, M.: Values and some technical problems in psychotherapy. Am. J. Orthopsychiat. 27:338-348, 1957.

CAMERON, N. & MARGARET, ANN: Behavior Pathology. Boston, Houghton-Mifflin, 1951.

CARPENTER, C. R.: A field study of the behavior and social relations of howling monkeys. Comp. Psychol. Monogr. 10:1-168, 1934.

CARTWRIGHT, D.: Emotional dimensions of group life. In: Feelings and Emotions (Raymert, M. L., Ed.) N. Y., McGraw-Hill, 1950.

— & ZANDER, A. (Eds.): Group Dynamics: Research and Theory. Evanston, Ill., Row Peterson, 1960.

CERLUTTI, V. & BINI, L.: L'eletrochoc. Arch. Gen. Neurol. Psychiat. 19:266, 1938.

COBB, S.: Foundations of Neuropsychiatry. (6th Ed.) Baltimore, Williams and Wilkins, 1958.

COLLINSON, J. B.: Brain model for clinicians, Arch. Gen. Psychiat. 11:495-502, 1964.

COOLEY, C. H.: Human Nature and the Social Order. N. Y., Scribner, 1922.

CRILE, G. W.: The Origin and Nature of the Emotions: Miscellaneous Papers. N. Y., W. B. Saunders, Co., 1915.

DEMENT, W.: Dream recall and eye movements during sleep in schizophrenics. J. N. M. D. 122:263-269, 1955.

—: Report of Current Research. Ass'n for the Psychological Study of Sleep. March 23, 1962.

—, & KLEITMAN, N.: Cyclic variations in EEG during sleep and their relation to eye movements, body motility and dreaming. Electroencephalog. Clin. Neurophysiol. 9:673-690, 1957.

DENBER, H. C. B. & MERLIS, S.: Studies on Mescaline. I. Action in Schizophrenic Patients. Psychiatric Quart. 29:421, 1955.

DENENBERG, V. H., ROSS, S., & BLUMENFIELD, M.: Behavior differences between mutant and unmutant mice. J. Comp. Physiol. Psychol. 56:290-293, 1963.

DEUTSCH, M.: A theory of cooperation and competition. Hum. Relat. 2:129-152, 1949.

—: The effects of competition on the group process. Hum. Relat. 2:129-152; 199-223, 1949.

—: Mechanism, organism, and society. Phil. Sci. 18:230-252, 1951.

—: Field theory in social psychology. In: Handbook of Social Psychology. Reading, Mass., Addison-Wesley Publ. Co., Pp. 181-222, 1954.

DEVEREUX, G.: Cultural factors in psychotherapy. J. Amer. Psychoanal. Ass'n. 1:629-655, 1953.

DOLLARD, J. & MILLER, N. E.: Personality and Psychotherapy: An Analysis in Terms of Learning, Thinking, and Culture. N. Y., McGraw-Hill, 1950.

DONIGER, S. (Ed.): Religion and Human Behavior. N. Y., Association Press, 1954.

DU BOIS, C.: Anthropology: its present interests. In: The Behavioral Sciences Today (Berelson, B., Ed.) N. Y., Basic Books, 1963.

DURKHEIM, E.: The Elementary Forms of the Religious Life. N. Y., Macmillan, 1915.

DURKIN, H.: The Group in Depth. N. Y., Int. Univ. Press, P. 26, 1964.

EIDUSON, B. T.: Brain mechanisms and psychotherapy. Amer. J. Psychiat. 115:203-210, 1958.

EINSTEIN, A.: Ideas and Opinions. N. Y., Crown, 1954.

— & INFELD, L.: The Evolution of Physics. N. Y., Simon & Schuster, 1938.

ERIKSON, E. H.: Childhood and Society. N. Y., Norton, 1950.

—: Identity and the Life Cycle. N. Y., Inter. Univ. Press, 1959.

ESCALONA, S. & HEIDER, C. M.: Prediction and Outcome. A Study in Child Development. N. Y., Basic Books, 1959.

FESTINGER, L.: Wish, expectation and group performance as factors influencing level of aspiration. J. Abn. Soc. Psychol. 37:184-200, 1942.

—: The role of group belongingness in a voting situation. Human Relat. 1:154-181, 1947.

—: A Theory of Cognitive Dissonance. Stanford Univ., Calif., 1957.

—: Cognitive dissonance. Sci. Amer. Vol. 207, No. 4, Pp. 93-102, 1962.

FOUREZIOS, N., HUTT, M. & GUETZKOW, H.: Measurement of self-oriented needs in discussion groups. J. Abn. & Soc. Psychol. 45:682-690, 1950.

FRANKL, V. E.: Arztliche Seelsorge. Vienna, Deuticke, 1948.

FREEDMAN, A. M.: Recent advances in the organic approach to psychosis. N. Y. S. J. Med. Pp. 2100-2113, July 1, 1960.

FREEMAN, W., & WATTS, J. W.: The frontal lobes and consciousness of the self. Psychosom. Med. 3:111, 1941.

FRENCH, J. R. P., Jr.: The disruption and cohesion of groups. J. Abn. Soc. Psychol. 36:361-377, 1941.

—: Organized and unorganized groups under fear and frustration. Univ. La. Stud. Child Welf. 20:299-308, 1944.

FREUD, S.: The Future of an Illusion. N. Y., Liveright, 1949.

GALLAGHER, J. J.: Educational methods with brain-damaged children. In: Current Psychiatric Therapies. (Masserman, J. H. Ed.) Vol. 2, N. Y., Grune & Stratton, Pp. 48-55, 1962.

GELHORN, E., & LOOFBOURROW, G. N.: Emotions and Emotional Disorders. N. Y., Harper & Row, 1963.

GESELL, A., & AMATRUDA, C.: Developmental Diagnosis: Normal and Abnormal Child Development, Clinical Methods and Pediatric Applications. 2nd Ed. N. Y., Hoeber, 1947.

GOLDSTEIN, K.: The Organism. N. Y., Am. Book Co., 1939.

GORDON, I. J.: Development and Learning. In: Behavioral Science Contributions To Psychiatry. (Regan, P. F. & Pattishall, E. G., Eds.) Boston, Little, Brown, & Co. Pp. 460-464, 1965.

GOUGH, H. G.: A sociological theory of psychotherapy. Amer. J. Sociol. 53:359-366, 1948.

GRINKER, R. R.: Editorial: Lysergic acid diethylamide. Arch. Gen. Psychiat. 8:425, 1963.

—: Psychiatry. J. A. M. A. 188:266-267, 1964.

GUNN, C. G., FRIEDMAN, M. & BYERS, S. O.: Effect of chronic hypothalamic stimulation upon cholesterol induced atheroschlerosis in rabbit. J. Clin. Invest. 30:1963-1972, 1960.

GUTHRIE, E. R.: The Psychology of Learning. N. Y., Harper, 1935.

HARE, A. P.: Handbook of Small Group Research. N. Y., Free Press of Glencoe, 1962.

HARLOW, H. F.: Motivational forces underlying learning. In: Learning Theory, Personality Theory, and Clinical Research—the Kentucky Symposium. N. Y., John Wiley & Sons, Pp. 35-52, 1954.

—: Primary Affectional Patterns In Primates. Amer. J. Orthopsychiat. 30:676-84, 1960.

—: The development of affectional patterns in infant monkeys. In: Determinants of Infant Behavior. (Foss, B. M. Ed.) N. Y., John Wiley & Sons, Pp. 75-97, 1961.

—: The Development of Learning in the Rhesus Monkey. Sci. Progr. 12:239-69, 1962.

—: The Effect of Rearing Conditions On Behavior. Bull. Menninger Clin. 26:213-24. Sept. 1962.

HARVEY, N. A.: Cybernetic approaches in medicine. I. Medical model making. N. Y. S. J. Med. 65:765, 1965a.

—: Cybernetic applications in medicine. N. Y. S. J. Med. 65:871, 1965 (b).

HEBB, D. O.: The Organization of Behavior: A Neuropsychological Theory. N. Y., Wiley, 1949.

—: The motivating effects of exteroceptive stimulation. Amer. Psychol. 13:109-113, 1958.

HEIDER, F.: Social perception and phenomenal causality. Psychol. Rev. 51:358-374, 1944.

HEINROTH, O.: Beitrage zur biologie, namentlich anthologie der anatiden. Verh. V. Int. Orn. Longr. Berlin, Pp. 589-702, 1910.

HESS, E. H.: Imprinting. Science. 130:133-141, 1959.

HILGARD, E. R.: Theories of Learning. N. Y., Appleton, 1956.

HILTNER, S.: Self Understanding. N. Y., Scribner, 1951.

HOCH, P. H.: Pharmacologically induced psychosis: In: American Handbook of Psychiatry. Vol. II, Arieti, S. (Ed.) N. Y., Basic Books, Pp. 1697-1708, 1959.

HOMANS, G. C.: The Human Group. N. Y., Harcourt, Brace & World, Inc. 1950.

HSU, F. L. K. (Ed.): Psychological Anthropology: Approaches to Culture and Personality. Homewood, Ill., Dorsey Press, 1961.

HULL, C. L.: Principles of Behavior. N. Y., Appleton-Century, 1943.

—: Essentials of Behavior, New Haven, Yale Univ. Press, 1951.

HUTCHINSON, H. W.: Village plantation life in Northeastern Brazil. Seattle, Univ. of Wash. Press, 1957.

—: Anthropology. In: Behavioral Science Contributions to Psychiatry. (Regan, P. F. & Pattishall, E. G., Jr. Eds.), Boston, Little, Brown & Co., Pp. 351-378, 1965.

HYMES, D. H.: The ethnography of speaking. In: Anthropology and Human Behavior. Wash., D. C., The Anthropol. Soc. of Wash., Pp. 13-53, 1962.

ITANI, J.: Paternal care in the wild Japanese monkey. J. Primatology. 2:61-93, 1959.

JARVIK, M. E., ABRAMSON, H. A. & HIRSCH, M. W.: Lysergic acid diethylamide (LSD-25) VI. Effect upon recall and recognition of various stimuli. J. Psychol. 39:443, 1955; VIII. Effect on arithmatic test performance. J. Psychol. 39:465, 1955.

JONES, E.: Essays in Applied Psychoanalysis. London, Hogarth Press, 1951.

JONES, M. B.: Behavior genetics. In: Behavioral Science Contribution To Psychiatry. (Regan, P. F. & Pattishall, E. G. Jr., Eds.) Boston, Little, Brown & Co., Pp. 233-269, 1965.

JOUVET, M.: Report of Current Research. Ass'n for the Psychophysiological Study of Sleep. March 23, 1962.

JUNG, C.: Modern Man In Search of a Soul. N. Y., Harcourt, 1933.

KALLMAN, F. J.: Expanding Goals of Genetics in Psychiatry. N. Y., Grune & Stratton, 1962.

KARDINER, A.: The Individual and His Society. N. Y., Columbia Univ. Press, 1939.

—: The Psychological Frontiers of Society. N. Y., Columbia Univ. Press, 1945.

KAWAMURA, S.: The process of sub-culture propagation among Japanese macaques. J. Primatology. 2:43-60, 1959.

KEELER, C. E. & KING, H. D.: Multiple effects of coat color genes in the Norway rat, with special reference to temperament and domestication. J. Comp. Psychol. 34: 241-251, 1942.

KEESING, F. M.: Cultural Anthropology. N. Y., Holt, Rinehart & Winston, 1959.

KETY, S. S.: Biochemical Theories of Schizophrenia. Internat. J. of Psychiat., 1:409-446, 1965.

KIERKEGAARD, S.: A Kierkegaard Anthology. (Bretall, R. Ed.) Princeton, N. J., Princeton Univ. Press, 1951.

KLEE, G. D.: Lysergic acid diethylamide (LSD-25) and ego functions. Arch. Gen. Psychiat. 8:461-474, 1963.

KOFFKA, K.: Principles of Gestalt Psychology. N. Y., Harcourt Brace, 1935.

KRAMER, S.: Ethology: the concept of fixed motor patterns. In: Behavioral Science Contributions to Psychiatry. (Regan, P. F. & Pattishall, E. G., Jr. Eds.), Boston, Little, Brown & Co., Pp. 269-302, 1965.

KROEBER, A. L.: The Nature of Culture. Chicago, Univ. of Chicago Press, 1952.

LABARRE, W.: The Influence of Freud on Anthropology. Amer. Imago. 15-275-328, 1958.

LEAKE, C. D.: Why search and research? J. A. M. A. 194:166-170, 1965.

LEEPER, R. W.: Cognitive processes. In: Handbook of Experimental Psychology. (S. S. Stevens Ed.) N. Y., Wiley, 1951.

LELAND, H. & SMITH, D. E.: Play Therapy with Mentally Subnormal Children. N. Y., Grune & Stratton, 1965.

LEIGHTON, A. H.: My Name is Legion. N. Y., Basic Books, 1959.

—: An Introduction to Social Psychiatry. Springfield, Ill., Thomas, 1960.

—: Psychiatric Disorder Among the Yoruba. Ithaca, Cornell Univ. Press, 1963.

LEWIN, K.: A Dynamic Theory of Personality. (Selected Papers) N. Y., McGraw-Hill, 1935.

—: Principles of Topological Psychology. N. Y., McGraw-Hill, 1936.

—: The conceptual representation and measurement of psychological forces. Contr. Psychol. Theor. 1: No. 4, 1938.

—: Frontiers in group dynamics. Human Relat. 1:2-38; 143-153, 1947.

—: Resolving Social Conflicts: Selected Papers On Group Dynamics. N. Y., Harper, 1948.

—: Field Theory in Social Science. N. Y., Harper, 1951.

LEWIS, O.: The Children of Sanchez, N. Y., Random House, 1963.

LIEBMAN, J. S. (Ed.): Psychiatry and Religion. Boston, Beacon, 1948.

LILLY, J.: Illustrative strategies for research on psychopathology in mental health. Symposium No. 2. In: Reports and Symposiums Group for the Advancement of Psychiatry, N. Y., Group, P. 13, 1955.

LINTON, R.: Culture and Mental Disorders. Springfield, Ill., Thomas, 1956.

LIPPITT, R., WATSON, J. & WESTLEY, B.: The Dynamics of Planned Change: A Comparative Study of Principles and Techniques. N. Y., Harcourt, Brace, 1958.

LONG, E. L., JR.: Religious Beliefs of American Scientists. Phila. Westminster, 1951.

LOOMIS, E. A.: Religion and Psychiatry. In: The Encyclopedia of Mental Health. (Deutsch, A. & Fishman, H. Eds.) N. Y. Encyclop. of Ment. Health, Pp. 1748-1759, 1963.

LORENZ, K.: The companion in the bird's world. Auk. 54:245-273, 1937.

—: The nature of instinct. In: Instinctive Behavior. (Schiller, C. H. Ed.) London, Methuen, Pp. 129-175, 1937.

—: King Solomon's Ring. London, Methuen, 1952.

—: The evolution of behavior. Sci. Amer. 199:67-78, 1958.

—: Man Meets Dog. Baltimore, Penguin (in preparation) 1965.

MACKAY, D. M. & McCULLOCH, W. S.: The limiting information capacity of a neuronal link. Bull. Math. Biophys. 14:127, 1952.

MAGOUN, H. W.: The ascending reticular system and wakefulness. In: Brain Mechanisms and Consciousness. Springfield, Ill., Thomas, Pp. 1-20, 1954.

—: Subcortical mechanisms for reinforcement. In: Moscow Colloquium on Electro-encephalography of Higher Nervous Activity. (Jasper, H. H. & Smirvov, G. D. Eds.) EEG Clin. Neurophysiol. Suppl. 13, 1960.

MAIER, H. W.: Three Theories of Child Development. N. Y., Harper & Row, Pp. 75-143, 1965.

MALINKOWSKI, B.: The Sexual Life of Savages in North-Western Melanesia, N. Y., Liveright, 1929.

MARUYAMA, M.: The second cybernetics: deviation-amplifying mutual causal processes. Am. Scientist, 51:164, 1963.

MASSERMAN, J. H.: Behavior and Neurosis. Chicago, Univ. Chicago Press, 1943.

—: Principles of Dynamic Psychiatry, Phila., Saunder, 1946.

—: The biodynamic approaches. In: American Handbook of Psychiatry, Vol. II, N. Y., Basic Books, Pp. 1680-1696, 1959.

—: Historical-comparative and experimental roots of short-term therapy. In: Short-term Psychotherapy. (Wolberg, L. R. Ed.) N. Y., Grune & Stratton, Pp. 23-50, 1965.

MAY, R.: The Meaning of Anxiety, N. Y., Ronald, 1950.

—: The existential approach. In: American Handbook of Psychiatry. (Arieti, S. Ed.) N. Y., Basic Books, Pp. 1348-1361, 1959.

McCLELLAND, D. C. ET AL.: Personality. N. Y., Holt, Rinehart & Winston, 1951.

—: Studies in Motivation, N. Y., Appleton, 1955.

—: Achieving Society, Princeton, Van Nostrand, 1961.

—: Roots of Consciousness. Princeton, Van Nostrand, 1964.

—: Talent and Society. Princeton, Van Nostrand (Paperbound) 1964.

—: Achievement Motive. N. Y., Appleton, 1953.

McDOUGALL, W.: Introduction To Social Psychology. Boston, Luce, 1908.

McGRAW, M. B.: The Neuromuscular Maturation of the Human Infant. N. Y., Hafner, Publ. Co., 1963.

McLEAN, P.: Psychiatry and philosophy. In: American Handbook of Psychiatry (Arieti, S. Ed.) N. Y., Basic Books, 1959.

MEAD, G. H.: A behavoristic account of the significant symbol. J. of Philos. Vol. 19, 1922.

—: Mind, Self and Society. Chicago, Univ. of Chicago Press, 1934.

MEAD, M.: From the South Seas. N. Y., Morrow, 1939.

—: Socialization and enculturation. Curr. Anthrop. 4:184-188, 1963.

MEDUNA, L. J.: Kie Konvulsionstherapie der Schizophrenie. Marhold, Halle, 1937.

MILLER, N. E.: Central stimulation and other new approaches to motivation and reward. Amer. Psychologist. 13:100-107, 1958.

MONIZ, E.: Tentatives operatoires dans le traitement de certaines psychoses. Paris, Masson, 1936.

MOORE, G. E.: Some Main Problems of Philosophy. London, Macmillan, 1953.

MORENO, J. L.: Who Shall Survive? A New Approach To The Problem of Human Interrelations. Nerv. & Ment. Dis. Publ. Co., Wash., D. C., 1934.

—: Foundations of sociometry, an introduction. Sociometry, 4:15-35, 1941.

—: Who Shall Survive? Foundations of Sociometry, Group Psychotherapy and Socio-drama. Beacon, N. Y., Beacon House, 1953.

MORGAN, C. T.: Physiological theory of drive. In: Psychology: A Study of Science. (Koch, S. Ed.) Vol. I, N. Y., McGraw-Hill, 1959.

MOWRER, O. H.: Learning theory and the Neurotic Paradox. Am. J. Orthopsychiat. 18:571, 1948.

MURPHY, G.: Personality: A Biosocial Approach to Origins and Structure. N. Y., Harper, 1947.

MURPHY, W. F.: The Tactics of Psychotherapy. The Application of Psychoanalytic Theory to Psychotherapy. N. Y., Inter. Univ. Press, 1965.

NEWMAN, H. H., FREEMAN, F. N. & HOLZINGER, K. J.: Twins: A Study of Heredity and Environment. Chicago, Univ. of Chicago Press, 1937.

NIEBUHR, R.: The Self and the Dramas of History, N. Y., Scribner, 1955.

OLDS, J.: Physiological mechanisms of reward. In: Nebraska Symposium on Motivation (Jones, M. R. Ed.) Lincoln, Neb., Univ. of Nebraska Press. Pp. 73-134, 1955.

OPLER, M. K. (ED.): Epidemiological studies of mental illness: methods and scope of the Midtown Study in New York. In: Symposium on Preventive and Social Psychiatry. Wash., D. C., Walter Reed Army Inst. of Research, Pp. 111-147, 1958.

—: Culture and Mental Health. N. Y., Macmillan, 1959.

—: Culture, Psychiatry and Human Values. Springfield, Ill., Thomas, 1965.

OSTOW, M.: The use of drugs for overcoming technical difficulties in psychoanalysis. Springfield, Ill., Charles C Thomas, 1960.

—: Pharmaceutical Agents In Psychoanalysis and Psychotherapy. N. Y., Basic Books, 1962.

PADILLA, E.: Up From Puerto Rico. N. Y., Columbia Univ. Press, 1958.

PAPEZ, J. W.: A proposed mechanism of emotion. Arch. Neurol. Psychiat. 38:725, 1937.

—: Neuroanatomy. In: American Handbook of Psychiatry. Vol. II, N. Y., Basic Books, Pp. 1585-1619, 1959.

PARSONS, T. & SHILS, E. A.: Toward a Theory of Action. Cambridge, Harvard Univ. Press, 1951.

PARSON, T. & BALES, R. F.: Socialization and Interaction. N. Y., Macmillan Co., 1950.

—: Family, Socialization and Interaction Process. Glencoe, Ill., Free Press, 1955.

PATTERSON, A. S.: Elecetrical and Drug Treatments. In: Psychiatry. London, Elsevier. Publ. Co., 1963.

PAVLOV, I. V.: Lectures on Conditioned Reflexes. Vol. I, N. Y., Internat. Publ. Co., 1928.

PEARSON, G. H. J.: Psychoanalysis and the education of the child. N. Y., Norton, 1954.

PEIPER, A.: A Cerebral Function in Infancy and Childhood. N. Y., Consultants Bureau, 1963.

PEIRCE, C. S.: In: The Philosophy of Peirce (Buchler, J.) N. Y., Harcourt, 1940.

PENFIELD, W.: Memory Mechanisms. Arch. Neurol. & Psychiat. 67:178-198, 1952.

— & ROBERTS, L.: Speech and Brain Mechanisms. Princeton, Princeton Univ. Press, 1959.

PIAGET, J.: The Child's Conception of Physical Causality. N. Y., Humanities Press, 1951.

—: The Origins of Intelligence in Children. N. Y., Inter. Univ. Press, 1952.

—: The genetic approach to the psychology of thought. J. Educ. Psychol. 52:275-281, 1961.

—: & INHELDER, B.: The Growth of Logical Thinking From Childhood to Adolescence. N. Y., Basic Books, 1958.

— & —: The Early Growth of Logic in the Child. N. Y., Harper & Row, 1964.

PRESTON, M. G. & HEINTZ, R. K.: Effects of participatory versus supervisory leadership on group judgment. J. Abn. & Soc. Psychol. 44:345, 1949.

PURPURA, D. P.: Electrophysiological analysis of psychotogenic drug action: I. Effect of LSD on specific afferent systems in the cat. A. M. A. Arch. Neurol. Psychiat. 75:122-131, 1956; II. General nature of lysergic acid diethylamide (LSD) action on central synapses. A. M. A. Arch. Neurol. Psychiat. 75:132-143, 1956.

RADO, S.: Relationship of short-term psychotherapy to developmental stages of maturation and stages of treatment behavior. In: Short-term Psychotherapy. (Wolberg, L. R. Ed.) N. Y., Grune & Stratton, Pp. 67-83, 1965.

RAPOPORT, A.: Mathematics and cybernetics. In: American Handbook of Psychiatry. Vol. II, N. Y., Basic Books, P. 1746, 1959.

REIK, T.: Dogma and Compulsion. N. Y., Inter. Univ. Press, 1951.

RIBBLE, M.: The Rights of Infants. N. Y., N. Y. Univ. Press, 1943.

ROCHE REPORT: Frontiers of Hospital Psychiatry. 1:1-2, 1964.

ROHEIM, G.: Psychoanalysis and Anthropology. N. Y., Int. Univ. Press, 1950.

ROIZIN, L.: Neuropathology. In: American Handbook of Psychiatry. Vol. II, N. Y., Basic Books, Pp. 1658-1679, 1959.

ROTHSTEIN, D. A.: Psychiatric implications of information theory. 13:87-94, 1965.

RUESCH, J.: Disturbed Communication. N. Y., Norton, 1957.

—: General theory of communication in psychiatry. In: American Handbook of Psychiatry. (Arieti, S. Ed.) N. Y., Basic Books, Pp. 894-908, 1959.

RYLE, G.: Philosophical Arguments. N. Y., Oxford University Press, 1945.

SAKEL, M.: Zur methodik hypoglykamie—behandlung von psychosen. Wien. Klin. Wschr. 49:1278, 1936.

SAPIR, E.: Why cultural anthropology needs the psychiatrist. Psychiatry. 1:7-12, 1937.

SANTAYANA, G.: The Life of Reason. 2nd Ed. N. Y., Scribner, 1948.

SARBIN, T. R.: Role theory. In: Handbook of Social Psychology. (Lindzey, G. Ed.) Reading, Mass. Addison-Wesley Publ. Co., Pp. 223-258, 1959.

SAVAGE, C.: Variations in ego feeling induced by D-lysergic acid diethylamide (LSD-25) Psychoanal. Rev. 43:1-16, 1955.

SCHEERER, M.: Cognitive theory. In: Handbook of Social Psychology. Reading, Mass., Addison-Wesley Publ. Co., Inc. P. 111, 1954.

SCHILDKRAUT, J. J.: The catecholamine hypothesis of affective disorders: a review of supporting evidence. Am. J. Psychiat. 122:509-522, 1965.

SELYE, H.: Stress, The Physiology and Pathology of Exposure to Stress. Montreal, Acta, 1950.

—: First Annual Report On Stress. Montreal, Acta, 1951.

—: Stress and psychiatry. Am. J. Psychiat. 113:423, 1956.

SHANNON, D. E.: A symbolic analysis of relay and switching circuits. Trans. Am. Inst. Elec. Engrs. 53:713-723, 1938.

SHANNON, D. E. & WEAVER, W.: The Mathematical Theory of Communication. Urbana, Ill., Univ. Ill. Press, 1949.

SHERIF, M.: The Psychology of Social Norms. N. Y., Harper, 1936.

SHERRINGTON, C. S.: The Brain and Its Mechanism. London, Cambridge, 1936.

SIMON, H. A. & NEWELL, A.: Information processing in computer and man. Am. Scientist, 52:281, 1964.

SKINNER, B. F.: The Behavior of Organisms. N. Y., Appleton-Century-Crofts, 1938.

SMITH, E. V.: Sociology. In: Behavioral Science Contributions To Psychiatry. (Regan, P. F. & Pattishall, Jr. E. G. Eds.) Boston, Little, Brown & Co. P. 390, 1965.

SNYDER, F.: The new biology of dreaming. A. M. A. Arch. Gen. Psychiat. 8:381-391, 1963.

SOKOLOV, E. N.: Neuronal models and the orienting influence. In: CNS and Behavior. Third Macy Conference (Brazier, M. A. B. Ed.) N. Y., Josiah Macy, Jr. Foundation, 1960.

SPENCE, K. W.: Behavior Theory and Conditioning. New Haven, Yale Univ. Press, 1956.

SPIEGEL, R.: Specific problems of communications in psychiatric conditions. In: American Handbook of Psychiatry. (Arieti, S. Ed.) N. Y., Basic Books, Pp. 909-949, 1959.

SPIRO, M. E.: Children of the Kibbutz. Cambridge, Mass., Harvard Univ. Press, 1958.

SROLE, L. & LANGNER, T. S.: Mental Health in the Metropolis: The Midtown Manhattan Study. N. Y., McGraw-Hill, 1962.

STACE, W. T.: Religion and the Modern Mind. Phila., Lippincott, 1952.

STERN, W.: General Psychology From the Personalistic Standpoint. N. Y., Macmillan, 1938.

STRAUSS, A. A., & LEHTINEN, L.: Psychopathology and Education of the Brain-injured Child. N. Y., Grune & Stratton, Vol. I, 1947, Vol. II, 1955.

Suzuki, D. T.: An Introduction to Zen Buddhism. London, Rider, 1947.
—: Mysticism: Christian and Buddhist. N. Y., Harper, 1957.

Thudichum, J. W. L.: A Treatise on the Chemical Constitution of the Brain. London, Balliere, Tindall and Co., 1884.
Tillich, P.: The Courage to Be. New Haven, Yale Univ. Press, 1952.
Tinbergen, N.: The Study of Instinct. London & N. Y., Oxford Univ. Press, 1951.
—: Bird Life. London & N. Y., Oxford Univ. Press, 1954.
—: Curious Naturalists. N. Y., Basic Books, 1959.
—: Herring Gull's World. rev. edit., N. Y., Basic Books, 1961.
—: On aims and methods of ethology. Z. Tierpsychol. 410-433, 1963.
Tolman, E. C.: Operational behaviorism and current trends in psychology. In: Proc. 25th Ann. Celebr. Inaug. Grad. Stud. (Hill, H. W. Ed.) Univ. S. Calif., Pp. 89-103, 1936.
Tooth, S.: Studies in Mental Illness in the Gold Coast. London, H. M. Stationary Office, 1960.
Toulmin, S.: The Place of Reason in Ethics. London, Cambridge, 1953.
Tylor, E. D.: Primitive Culture. London, John Murray, 1871.
Vogt, C. & Vogt, O.: Importance of neuro-anatomy in the field of neuropathology. Neurology. 1:205, 1951.
Von Bertalanffy, L.: An outline of general systems theory. Brit. J. Phil. Sci. 1:134, 1950 a.
—: The theory of open systems in physics and biology. Science 111:23, 1950 b.
Vygotsky, L. S.: Thought and Language. Cambridge, M. I. T. Press, 1962.

Wallace, A. F. C.: Culture and Personality. N. Y., Random House, 1961.
—: Mental Illness, biology and culture. In: Psychological Anthropology: Approaches to Culture and Personality. Homewood, Ill., Dorsey Press, Pp. 255-295, 1961.
—: The New Culture and Personality. In: Anthropology and Human Behavior. Wash., D. C. The Anthropological Society of Wash., 1962.
Watts, A. W.: The Way of Zen. N. Y., Pantheon, 1957.
Weil, G. M., Metzner, R. & Leary, T. (Eds.): The Psychedelic Reader. N. Y., University Books, 1965.
Weintraub, W., Silverstein, A., & Klee, G. D.: The effect of LSD on the associative processes. N. Nerv. Ment. Dis. 128:409-414, 1959.
—: The "correction" of deviant responses on a word association test: a measure of the defensive functions of the ego. Arch. Gen. Psychiat. 3:17-20, 1960.
Weiss, P.: From cell to molecule. In: Molecular Control of Cellular Activity (Allen, J. M. Ed.) N. Y., McGraw-Hill, Pp. 1-72, 1962.
Werner, H.: Comparative psychology of mental development. Chicago, Follett, 1948.
Wheeler, W. M.: Ethological observations on an American ant. (Leptothorax Emersoni Wheeler) Arch. Psychol. Neurol. 2:1-21, 1903.
—: Ants, Their Structure, Development and Behavior. N. Y., Columbia Univ. Press, 1910.
Whitehead, A. N.: Science and the Modern World. N. Y., Macmillan, 1925.
Whiting, B. B.: Six Cultures: Studies in Child Rearing. N. Y., John Wiley & Sons, 1963.
Whitman, C. O.: The Behavior of Pigeons. Vol. III, Carnegie Institution of Washington, 1919.
Wiener, N.: Cybernetics. N. Y., John Wiley & Sons, Inc., 1948.

WILDER, J.: Modern Psychotherapy and the law of initial values. In: Amer. J. of Psychother., 12:199, 1953.

WISDOM, J. O.: Foreword. In: The Structure of Metaphysics. (Lazerowitz, M.) N. Y., Humanities, 1955.

WITTKOWER, E. D. & RIN, H.: Transcultural psychiatry. Arch. Gen. Psychiat. 13:387-394, 1965.

WOLF, S.: A new view of disease. J.A.M.A. 184:129-130, 1963.

WOLPERT, E. A. & TROSMAN, H.: Studies in psychophysiology of dreams. A. M. A. Arch. Neurol. Psychiat. 79:603-606, 1958.

YERKES, R. M. & YERKES, A. W.: The Great Apes. New Haven, Yale Univ. Press, 1929.

ZUCKERMAN, S.: The Social Life of Monkeys and Apes. London, Routledge & Kegan Paul, 1932.

Author Index

190

Subject Index